1 SAMUEL

The Lives of Samuel and Saul

John MacArthur

THOMAS NELSON
Since 1798

MacArthur Bible Studies

1 Samuel: The Lives of Samuel and Saul

Published in Nashville, Tennessee, by Nelson Books, an imprint of Thomas Nelson. Nelson Books and Thomas Nelson are registered trademarks of HarperCollins Christian Publishing, Inc.

Originally published in association with the literary agency of Wolgemuth & Associates, Inc. Original layout, design, and writing assistance by Gregory C. Benoit Publishing, Old Mystic, Connecticut.

"Unleashing God's Truth, One Verse at a Time®" is a trademark of Grace to You. All rights reserved.

Thomas Nelson, Inc. titles may be purchased in bulk for educational, business, fundraising, or sales promotional use. For information, please e-mail SpecialMarkets@ThomasNelson.com.

Scripture quotations are taken from *The New King James Version*. © 1982 by Thomas Nelson, Inc. Used by permission. All rights reserved.

Some material from the Introduction, "Keys to the Text" and "Exploring the Meaning" sections taken from *The MacArthur Bible Commentary*, John MacArthur, Copyright © 2005 Thomas Nelson Publishers.

ISBN 978-0-7180-3472-6

First Printing January 2016 / Printed in the United States of America

HB 12.11.2023

CONTENTS

INTRODUCTION

After the Israelites settled into the Promised Land, a series of judges led the people for more than four hundred years. However, the Israelites eventually grew bored with that system—even though it had been the Lord's design. As the people looked around at the pagan nations of Canaan, they saw that everybody else had a king—and they wanted one of their own. Eventually, the Lord would grant their demands, but He would also warn that a king would bring with him a great deal of suffering for the nation.

In these twelve studies, we will examine the biblical events depicted in the book of 1 Samuel. We will become acquainted with the high priest Eli, and his two wicked sons, Hophni and Phinehas. We will meet Eli's young protégé, named Samuel, and examine his faithfulness. We will get to know Samuel's mother, Hannah, and learn why the young boy was brought up by a priest in the temple rather than by his family at home. We will be introduced to Saul, Israel's first king, and watch his sad decline. Finally, we will meet Saul's successor, David, who stood in marked contrast to his predecessor.

Through it all, we will learn some precious truths about the character of God, and we will see His great faithfulness in keeping His promises. We will learn, as did the prophet Samuel and King David, what it means to walk by faith.

TITLE

First and Second Samuel were considered one book in the earliest Hebrew manuscripts. They were later divided into two books by the translators of the

Greek version, known as the Septuagint. This division was later followed by the Latin Vulgate, English translations, and modern Hebrew Bibles. The earliest Hebrew manuscripts titled the one book *Samuel*, after the man God used to establish the kingship in Israel.

AUTHOR AND DATE

Jewish tradition ascribed the writing of Samuel to the prophet himself or to Samuel, Nathan, and Gad (based on 1 Chronicles 29:29). However, Samuel cannot be the writer, because his death is recorded in 1 Samuel 25:1, before the events associated with David's reign take place. Further, Nathan and Gad were prophets of the Lord during David's lifetime and would not have been alive when the book was written. Thus, though the written records of these three prophets could have been used for information in the writing of 1 and 2 Samuel, the human author of these books is unknown. The work comes to the reader as an anonymous writing.

The books of Samuel contain no clear indication of the date of composition. However, it is clear the author wrote them after the division of the kingdom between Israel and Judah in 931 BC due to the many references to Israel and Judah as distinct entities. Also, the statement concerning Ziklag's belonging "to the kings of Judah to this day" in 1 Samuel 27:6 gives clear evidence of a post-Solomonic date of writing. There is no such clarity concerning how late the date of writing could be, but most likely it was penned before the exile during the period of the divided kingdom (c. 931–722 BC).

BACKGROUND AND SETTING

The majority of the action in 1 and 2 Samuel takes place in and around the central highlands of Israel. The nation was largely concentrated in an area that ran about ninety miles from the hill country of Ephraim in the north to the hill country of Judah in the south, and between fifteen to thirty-five miles east to west. The major cities of 1 and 2 Samuel were found in these central highlands: Shiloh, the residence of Eli and the tabernacle; Ramah, the hometown of Samuel; Gibeah, the headquarters of Saul; Bethlehem, the birthplace of David; Hebron, David's capital when he ruled over Judah; and Jerusalem, the ultimate "city of David."

The events in 1 and 2 Samuel occurred between the years c. 1105 BC (the birth of Samuel in 1 Samuel 1:1–28) and c. 971 BC (the last words of David in 2 Samuel 23:1–7). Thus, the books span about 135 years of history. During those years, Israel was transformed from a loosely knit group of tribes under judges to a united nation under the reign of a centralized monarchy. The books primarily examine the lives of Samuel (c. 1105–1030 BC); Saul, who reigned c. 1051–1011 BC; and David, who was king of the united monarchy (c. 1011–971 BC).

HISTORICAL AND THEOLOGICAL THEMES

As 1 Samuel begins, Israel was at a low point spiritually. The priesthood was corrupt, the ark of the covenant was not at the tabernacle, idolatry was being practiced, and the judges were dishonest. Through the influence of Samuel and David, these conditions were reversed.

During the years narrated in 1 and 2 Samuel, the great empires of the ancient world were in a state of weakness. Neither Egypt nor the Mesopotamian powers, Babylon and Assyria, were threats to Israel at this time. The two nations most hostile to the Israelites were the Ammonites to the east and the Philistines to the west. The Ammonites were descendants of Lot (see Genesis 19:38) who lived on the Transjordan plateau. The major contingent of the Philistines had migrated from the Aegean islands and Asia Minor in the twelfth century BC. After being denied access to Egypt, they settled among other Philistines along the Mediterranean coast of Palestine. They controlled the use of iron, which gave them a decided military and economic advantage over Israel.

There are four predominant theological themes in 1 and 2 Samuel. The first is the Davidic covenant. The books are literally framed by two references to the "anointed" king in the prayer of Hannah (see 1 Samuel 2:10) and the song of David (see 2 Samuel 22:51). This is a reference to the Messiah, the King who would triumph over the nations who are opposed to God. According to the Lord's promise, this Messiah would come through the line of David and establish David's throne forever (see 2 Samuel 7:12–16). The events of David's life recorded in Samuel foreshadow the actions of David's greater Son (Christ) in the future.

A second theme is the sovereignty of God. One example is the birth of Samuel in response to Hannah's prayer (see 1 Samuel 9:17; 16:12–13). Also, in relation to David, it is particularly evident that nothing can frustrate God's plan to have him rule over Israel.

A third theme is the work of the Holy Spirit in empowering people for divinely appointed tasks. The Spirit of the Lord came on both Saul and David after their anointing as king (see 1 Samuel 10:10; 16:13). The power of the Holy Spirit brought forth prophecy (see 10:6) and victory in battle (see 11:6).

A fourth theme centers on the personal and national effects of sin. The sins of Eli and his sons resulted in their deaths (see 1 Samuel 2–4). The lack of reverence for the ark of the covenant led to the death of a number of Israelites (see 1 Samuel 6:19; 2 Samuel 6:6–7). Saul's disobedience resulted in the Lord's judgment, and he was rejected as king over Israel (see 1 Samuel 13 and 15). In addition, though David was forgiven for his sin of adultery and murder after his confession (see 2 Samuel 12:13), he still suffered the inevitable and devastating consequences of his sin (see 12:14).

INTERPRETIVE CHALLENGES

The books of 1 and 2 Samuel contain a number of interpretive issues that have been widely discussed. The first issue is *which of the ancient manuscripts is closest to the original autograph.* The standard Hebrew (Masoretic) text has been relatively poorly preserved, and the Septuagint often differs from it. Thus, the exact reading of the original autograph in places is hard to determine (see, for example, 1 Samuel 13:1). For this study, the Masoretic text will be assumed to represent the original text unless there is a grammatical or contextual impossibility, which will account for many of the numerical discrepancies.

A second issue is *whether Samuel is ambivalent to the establishment of the human kingship in Israel.* It is claimed that while 1 Samuel 9–11 presents a positive view of the kingship, 1 Samuel 8 and 12 are strongly anti-monarchial. It is preferable, however, to see the book as presenting a balanced perspective of the human kingship. While the desire of Israel for a king was acceptable (see Deuteronomy 17:15), their reason for wanting a king showed a lack of faith in the Lord.

A third issue is *how to explain the bizarre behavior of the prophets.* It is commonly held that 1 and 2 Samuel present the prophets as ecstatic speakers with bizarre behavior, just like the pagan prophets of the other nations. However, there is nothing in the text that is inconsistent with seeing the prophets as communicators of divine revelation, at times prophesying with musical accompaniment.

A fourth issue is *how the Holy Spirit ministered before Pentecost*. Passages about the Spirit's ministry, such as 1 Samuel 10:6, 10; 11:6; 16:13–14; 19:20, 23; and 2 Samuel 23:2, do not describe salvation in the New Testament sense but as an empowering by the Lord for His service (see also Judges 3:10; 6:34; 11:29; 13:25; 14:6, 19; 15:14).

A final issue concerns *the identity of the "distressing spirit from the Lord"* (see, for example, 1 Samuel 16:14). Was this a personal being (that is, a demon) or a spirit of discontent created by God in the heart? Traditionally, this spirit has been viewed as a demon.

ISRAEL DURING SAMUEL AND SAUL

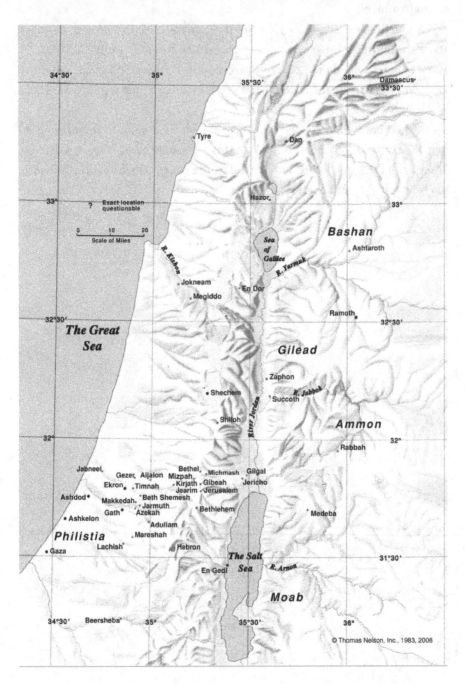

34°30'   35°   35°30'   36°   Damascus 33°30'

Tyre   Dan

33°   ? Exact location questionable   Hazor   Bashan   33°

0   10   20   Sea of Galilee   Ashtaroth
Scale of Miles   R. Yarmuk

R. Kishon   Jokneam   En Dor   Ramoth
32°30'   Megiddo   32°30'

The Great Sea   Gilead

Zaphon
Shechem   R. Jabbok
Succoth
Shiloh   River Jordan
32°   Ammon   32°

Rabbah

Jabneel   Bethel   Michmash   Gilgal
Gezer   Aijalon   Mizpah   Jericho
Ekron   Kirjath   Gibeah
Timnah   Jearim   Jerusalem
Ashdod   Makkedah   Beth Shemesh   Medeba
Gath   Jarmuth   Bethlehem
Ashkelon   Azekah
Adullam
Philistia   Mareshah
Gaza   Lachish   Hebron
The Salt
En Gedi   Sea   R. Arnon   31°30'

Moab
34°30'   Beersheba   35°   35°30'   36°

© Thomas Nelson, Inc., 1983, 2008

HANNAH'S VOW

1 Samuel 1:1–2:21

DRAWING NEAR

What are some types of "vows" that people make to God? In what kinds of situations do they tend to make these vows?

_____

_____

_____

THE CONTEXT

We open our study at the close of the time known in Israel as the period of the judges. The judges were individuals whom the Lord raised up at various times and places during a period of some 350 years, beginning soon after Joshua led the people into Canaan. The judges exercised limited authority over portions of Israel, with most of them only dealing with one or two of the twelve tribes. They frequently led Israel into battle against political enemies, and some acted as judges in civil disputes as well.

As we will see in future studies, a man named Samuel would become Israel's final judge and God's prophet to His people. He would be a great man of God and serve the Lord faithfully from his earliest childhood until the day he died. But where did such a man come from? What shaped him to become a great man of God? As the old saying goes, the apple does not fall far from the tree; so who were the parents who prepared him for a lifetime of service?

In this study, we will meet Samuel's parents—notably his mother, Hannah. In Samuel's day, it was considered a disgrace for a woman to be barren. People understood children to be a gift from God, and they took that concept a step further to assume that a wife who bore no children must be under the Lord's discipline for some sin. This assumption was not true (at least not in Hannah's case), but that did not stop people from treating her with contempt when she found herself unable to bear children to her husband.

To make matters much worse, Hannah's husband had two wives—and the other wife had borne him many sons and daughters. As was common in such polygamous households, the two wives began to resent one another, and "the other woman" took every opportunity to ridicule Hannah for her inability to produce an heir. In general, Hannah found herself the object of great scorn and verbal abuse because of her barrenness, and her heart was filled with grief. But then, one day, she took her sorrows to the Lord—and that changed everything.

KEYS TO THE TEXT

Read 1 Samuel 1:1–2:11, noting the key words and phrases indicated below.

> AN UNHAPPY FAMILY: *Elkanah has two wives, Hannah and Peninnah. Peninnah has numerous children, but Hannah is barren. This produces strife in the home.*

1:1. A CERTAIN MAN: This verse is similar to the one that introduces the birth of Samson (see Judges 13:2). The strong comparison also highlights the similarities between the lives of Samson and Samuel. Both men were judges over Israel, fighters of the Philistines, and lifelong Nazirites.

RAMATHAIM ZOPHIM: Also called Ramah, located just south of Mizpah.

ELKANAH: Meaning "God has created."

2. HE HAD TWO WIVES: Monogamy was God's intention for mankind from the time of creation (see Genesis 2:24). Polygamy was a common practice in the ancient Middle East, but the Scriptures never endorse it.

HANNAH HAD NO CHILDREN: Hannah's name means "grace," and her life became a model of God's grace. It was considered a disgrace in her day for a woman to be childless, as it was interpreted by the world at large as a sign of God's disfavor. It only made Hannah's burden greater to be forced to live with another woman who had borne her husband numerous children. The same situation caused much grief in Jacob's household (see Genesis 29–30).

PENINNAH: Her name means "ruby."

3. THIS MAN WENT UP FROM HIS CITY YEARLY: All Israelite men were required to attend three annual feasts at the central sanctuary (see Deuteronomy 16:1–17).

THE LORD OF HOSTS: The word hosts can refer to human armies (see Exodus 7:4), celestial bodies (see Deuteronomy 4:19), or heavenly creatures (see Joshua 5:14). The name emphasizes God's sovereignty over all creation, including the daily affairs of human beings.

IN SHILOH: Located about twenty miles north of Jerusalem in Ephraim. The tabernacle and ark of the covenant resided there.

5. A DOUBLE PORTION: This was a public display of favor and honor. Elkanah may have been intending to comfort Hannah in her barrenness, but such blatant favoritism could only produce more problems within the home.

THE LORD HAD CLOSED HER WOMB: The Lord had deliberately prevented Hannah from bearing children, just as He had done with Sarah and Rachel. He is sovereign over every event in our lives, even those things we might ascribe to natural causes.

6. HER RIVAL: That is, Peninnah. It is telling that she is not described as "Elkanah's other wife" or "Hannah's family member." As this situation shows, disregarding the Lord's intended family structure only brings heartache and rivalry. Peninnah probably taunted and provoked Hannah because their husband was so open in his favoritism.

HANNAH TURNS TO THE LORD: *Elkanah takes his entire family to the temple in Shiloh to attend one of the annual festivals. While there, Hannah pours out her grief before the Lord.*

7. SHE WENT UP TO THE HOUSE OF THE LORD: The law demanded all men of Israel to appear before the Lord at His temple on three occasions each year. Many took their families with them, though they were not required to

do so. The fact that Elkanah also provided offerings for his wives, sons, and daughters indicates he was a godly man who taught his children the ways of the Lord.

8. WHY DO YOU WEEP: Elkanah probably intended to comfort and encourage his wife, yet he could hardly have comprehended her sense of sadness and despair. His love undoubtedly did comfort her, yet it was also a cause of the tension between her and Peninnah. In the long run, Elkanah's role as a loving husband did not remove Hannah's longing for a son.

10. BITTERNESS OF SOUL: Hannah's sorrow was so great that her life felt like a bitter burden. She did not make a public display of her sorrow, however, but poured out her heart in prayer to the Lord, the only One who could heal her heartache. Notice also she "wept in anguish" in God's presence, rather than attempting some level of stoicism. The Lord wants His children to pour out their hearts to Him honestly, even when they are filled with sorrow.

11. SHE MADE A VOW: It is a serious thing to make a vow to the Lord. It should not be undertaken lightly, for God expects His people to fulfill their vows.

NO RAZOR SHALL COME UPON HIS HEAD: Hannah was referring to the vows of a Nazirite, a young man who voluntarily took on specific strictures for a time of dedicated service to the Lord. The Nazirite did not cut his hair, refrained from wine, and avoided any contact with dead bodies. The Nazirite vows were usually taken for several weeks or even a few months at most. Hannah was dedicating her unborn son to a *lifetime* Nazirite vow—dedicating him fully to the Lord's service and voluntarily giving up her rights and expectations as the boy's mother.

13. ELI THOUGHT SHE WAS DRUNK: This is a sad introduction to Eli, the high priest at Shiloh. He should have expected that the people who gathered in the temple were there to worship the Lord. However, his own sons had corrupted the temple with their wickedness, and it may even have been fairly common for Eli to see people acting with irreverence during times of worship. He assumed the worst because his own heart was not dedicated to the Lord's service.

15. I AM A WOMAN OF SORROWFUL SPIRIT: It is tragic that Hannah was forced to defend her private prayers before the high priest himself—the one man who ought to have been her intercessor and defender.

16. OUT OF THE ABUNDANCE OF MY COMPLAINT: Hannah was doing exactly what the Lord wanted her to do by pouring out her heart's burden before Him. God wants the same from us today. What's more, as Christians we have the full assistance of the Holy Spirit in pouring out our concerns to the Father (see Romans 8:26).

THE LORD ANSWERS: Once Eli understands the situation, he blesses Hannah, and she takes that as a promise from the Lord that He will grant her plea.

18. HER FACE WAS NO LONGER SAD: Hannah demonstrated great faith at this moment. She had poured out her heart to the Lord and had received an answer. She accepted Eli's word of blessing as a promise from the Lord, demonstrating her own faith in His faithful character. In this she was like Abraham, who believed the promise of God that he would receive a son.

20. SAMUEL: The name means "name of God," but it also sounds similar to the Hebrew word meaning "heard of God." Hannah recognized that her son was a direct gift from the Lord; that He had heard her prayer and had granted her request. She also did not forget her vow, and she fulfilled it faithfully.

21. AND HIS VOW: Elkanah had the power to nullify his wife's vow according to God's law (see Numbers 30:6–15), yet here we find he knew of her vow and supported it fully. In God's eyes, Hannah's vow became binding on her husband as well, and Elkanah recognized his solemn responsibility to see that it was fulfilled. In this, he demonstrated his deep love for his wife far more than his words of encouragement could have done.

22. NOT UNTIL THE CHILD IS WEANED: Jewish custom at the time was to breastfeed a child until he was two or three years old.

REMAIN THERE FOREVER: Notice Hannah did not say, "He will remain in the Lord's presence all his life." She understood the Lord's children will be in His presence far beyond this earthly life and enjoy His company for all eternity.

24. THE CHILD WAS YOUNG: Samuel was probably around three years old when he entered the Lord's service at the temple.

28. I ALSO HAVE LENT HIM TO THE LORD: This does not mean Hannah was permitting the Lord to borrow her son for a time but that she was devoting him fully to the Lord's service with no expectation of receiving him back again.

HANNAH'S SONG: Hannah is so overjoyed at the Lord's miraculous answer to her request that she pours out her heart once again, this time in praise and joy.

2:1. MY HEART REJOICES IN THE LORD: What a majestic contrast between this prayer and Hannah's earlier one! Her heart was filled to overflowing once again, but this time with praise and adoration. Her prayer was actually a song, or psalm, of praise to the Lord's faithfulness and power, and it bears many similarities to the song Mary sang after receiving the news that she would bear the Son of God (see Luke 1:46–55).

3. LET NO ARROGANCE COME FROM YOUR MOUTH: The Lord humbles those who raise themselves against Him and raises those who humble themselves before His will. We see this in the attitudes of Hannah and Peninnah. Peninnah gloried in her fertility as though she were responsible for her ability to bear children, while Hannah recognized such things were from the Lord and took her sorrow and desires to Him. Those who submit to God's sovereignty shall be blessed, while those who arrogantly follow their own will shall be humbled.

5. THE BARREN HAS BORNE SEVEN: Hannah gave birth to a total of six children (the *seven* here is poetic, not intended as prophecy). She asked the Lord for one child, and He poured out an abundance in reply. God loves to have His children turn to Him for all their needs, and He loves "to do exceedingly abundantly above all that we ask or think" (Ephesians 3:20). Peninnah became "feeble" by comparison; she may have born sons and daughters, but it was Hannah's son who became Israel's prophet and judge, the anointer of kings.

9. BY STRENGTH NO MAN SHALL PREVAIL: Those who trust in their own power and wisdom shall be broken, but those who trust fully in the Lord shall find that He fights on their behalf. Hannah placed her faith in the Lord's power, and she was not disappointed.

18. WEARING A LINEN EPHOD: Samuel apparently began to assist Eli in his duties as soon as he could walk and talk. Eli evidently had a miniature ephod (a sleeveless outer vest that extended to the hips) made to fit young Samuel.

19. HIS MOTHER USED TO MAKE HIM A LITTLE ROBE: The touching picture shows us that Hannah never stopped loving Samuel as her firstborn son. She continued to minister to his needs, and by doing so she participated in his ministry before the Lord.

21. THE LORD VISITED HANNAH: The Lord eventually blessed Hannah with six children: four sons and two daughters.

UNLEASHING THE TEXT

1) Why did Peninnah abuse Hannah about her childlessness? What did this reveal about her character? About Hannah's character? What did it reveal about their home life?

_____

_____

_____

_____

2) Why did Eli think Hannah was drunk? What does this reveal about Eli's character? About Hannah's grief?

_____

_____

_____

_____

3) In what ways did Hannah remain a good mother to Samuel? What did her sacrifice cost her? What did she gain?

_____

_____

_____

_____

4) How did Hannah describe God in her song? What are some of the things she says that the Lord does?

_____

_____

_____

EXPLORING THE MEANING

God is the author of all life. Hannah recognized it was the Lord's responsibility to provide her with children or withhold them as He saw fit. Her childlessness caused her deep grief because people in her day generally viewed a lack of children as a sign of God's disapproval. This view in itself underscores the fact that it is God's choice to bestow children or to withhold them.

In modern times, we hear a lot about "choice" when it comes to children. Ironically, that choice is often a euphemism for abortion—the wanton slaying of a God-given life within a woman's womb. This idea implies that human life is a choice made by a man or a woman, but the Scriptures are clear that God is the one who gives life; the choice is His alone to make.

Children are a blessing from God, not a burden or a "lifestyle" choice. The married couple who gains a child has great cause for rejoicing, while the childless couple should pour out their request before the Lord as Hannah did. "Behold, children are a heritage from the LORD, the fruit of the womb is a reward. Like arrows in the hand of a warrior, so are the children of one's youth. Happy is the man who has his quiver full of them; they shall not be ashamed, but shall speak with their enemies in the gate" (Psalm 127:3–5).

God's sovereignty over life does not stop at conception. Hannah sings that "the LORD kills and makes alive; He brings down to the grave and brings up" (1 Samuel 2:6). In the same way God divinely and sovereignly causes pregnancy, He is also the one ultimately in control of how long people live. Beyond that, Hannah describes the Lord as the One who not only determines a person's lifespan but also is sovereign over eternity. He is the One who sends people to the grave as well as the One who brings people to everlasting life.

The Lord uses the weak things of the world for His glory. Throughout history, God has routinely chosen the unexpected and the unlikely to be recipients of His grace. He chose Abraham and Sarah, who by all accounts were too old to have children, and promised they would produce a nation. He chose the Israelites, who were weaker than all their neighbors and in captivity, to become His people. This same way of working is seen in Hannah's life. She can declare from personal experience that the Lord is the One who blesses the needy and humbles the proud (see 1 Samuel 2:7–8).

This is how God still works today. In His mysterious way, He has chosen "the foolish things of the world to shame the wise, and . . . the weak things of the world to shame the things which are mighty" (1 Corinthians 1:27). God does this to prove there is not a human explanation behind the gospel. It is entirely supernatural.

There was any number of Israelite wives whom God could have used to bring Samuel into the world. But God wanted a woman who was desperately dependent on Him, so he chose Hannah, and not Peninnah, to bring forth Samuel. God receives more glory from being served by those who are absolutely dependent on Him.

The Lord loves to have His children pour out their hearts to Him. Hannah suffered a great deal because of a situation that was beyond her control. It was not her fault she had no children, but it caused her much heartache. To make matters worse, Peninnah constantly mocked her and reminded her day after day of her barrenness. She bore the humiliation and sorrow until her heart reached the point that it must certainly have broken from the pain.

Then Hannah found the solution. It was not some wonder drug that opened her womb, nor did she turn to the learning of science. Indeed, she stopped turning to others for her answer and instead turned to the Lord. She poured out her heart without attempting to clothe her emotions in fancy prayers or stilted words. She told the Lord her grief, expressed her ache and sorrow, and pleaded with Him for an answer—and the Lord was pleased with her prayer.

Our Father has not changed; He still delights in the honest, open prayers of His children. He wants us to find all our answers in Him and tell Him our deepest desires and most private pains. Jesus promised that God would answer the prayers of those who pray according to His will: "Most assuredly, I say to you, whatever you ask the Father in My name He will give you . . . Ask, and you will receive, that your joy may be full" (John 16:23–24). John later wrote that "if our heart does not condemn us, we have confidence toward God. And whatever we ask we receive from Him, because we keep His commandments and do those things that are pleasing in His sight" (1 John 3:21–22).

REFLECTING ON THE TEXT

5) Why did Hannah pour out her grief to the Lord? What result did she expect from her prayers? What does this reveal about her trust in God?

_____

_____

_____

_____

6) Why did Hannah promise to devote her son to the Lord's service? Why did the Lord wait until that moment to grant her request?

_____

_____

_____

_____

7) What does this passage reveal about God's role in childbearing? About a parent's role?

_____

_____

_____

8) How does Hannah's song describe God's sovereignty? How is Hannah's understanding of God's control different from how the world views God?

_____

_____

_____

PERSONAL RESPONSE

9) What promises have you made to the Lord? To other people? How well are you keeping those promises?

_____

_____

_____

10) How do the principles in this passage reveal the problem of viewing abortion as a "choice" made by human parents? How does the Lord view an "unwanted" pregnancy?

_____

_____

_____

2

A VISIT FROM GOD

1 Samuel 3:1–21

DRAWING NEAR

What is a difficult piece of news that you have had to deliver to someone?
How did you go about communicating that news?

_____

_____

_____

THE CONTEXT

In the previous study, we saw how a woman named Hannah vowed to dedicate her firstborn son to the Lord. When the child, whom she named Samuel, was born and reached the age of two or three years old, she fulfilled her vow and brought him to Shiloh, where he ministered to the Lord before Eli the priest. In time, Samuel would become not only Israel's last judge but also the first prophet God would appoint to speak His words to the *entire* nation.

By the time the events in today's study unfold, Samuel had been serving Eli—whom he revered as a father—for many years. However, while Samuel was growing "in favor both with the LORD and men" (1 Samuel 2:26), Eli's two sons, who also served as priests, were growing in wickedness. They abused their privileges when it came to partaking of the portion of the sacrifice given to the priests (see Deuteronomy 18:3) and even engaged in sexual relationships with the women who served at the tabernacle. Because of their wickedness, God determined the house of Eli would forfeit their priesthood (see 1 Samuel 2:27–36).

Given this state of Israel's spiritual leadership, it is little wonder that "the word of the LORD was rare in those days" (3:1). However, all that would change in the dark hours of one night when the Lord appeared to the young boy Samuel and called him by name. Despite some initial confusion on his part, Samuel would eventually realize that God was calling out directly to him. When he answered the Lord with a willing heart and obediently relayed God's message to Eli about his sons in spite of his fears, it forever changed the course of his life.

From that moment to the day of his death, Samuel served the Lord as His prophet in the land of Israel. His life stands out because he served God fully and willingly—with his *whole heart.*

Keys to the Text

Read 1 Samuel 3:1–21, noting the key words and phrases indicated below.

> YOUNG SAMUEL: *When we meet Samuel again, he is a youth living in the temple, sleeping next to the ark of God and serving the Lord full-time.*

3:1. THE BOY SAMUEL: Samuel was probably about twelve at this time, or possibly in his early teens.

ELI: His name means "exalted is the Lord." He was the high priest at the time, but his two sons were ungodly men.

THE WORD OF THE LORD WAS RARE IN THOSE DAYS: Samuel lived at the end of the period of the judges, which lasted approximately 350 years after Joshua led the people into Canaan. Prophetic revelation from the Lord was extremely limited during those years, as the Lord had chosen to reveal Himself specifically to individuals whom He called to become judges, or leaders, in Israel. The Lord was about to change His ways of revealing Himself to His people, however, by making His word known more frequently in Israel through His prophet Samuel.

3. BEFORE THE LAMP OF GOD WENT OUT IN THE TABERNACLE: The golden lampstand was located in the Holy Place of the tabernacle. It was lit at twilight and kept burning until morning (see Exodus 27:20–21). The Lord called Samuel to his prophetic ministry in the hours before dawn.

> GOD CALLS SAMUEL: *Samuel has served the Lord all his young life, but he still does not have a personal knowledge of God's character. This will soon change.*

4. HERE I AM: Young Samuel's response to the Lord's call gives us some early insight into his character. As he grew in his role as prophet, he learned to listen for the Lord's voice and was always quick to respond. Part of the reason "the word of the LORD was rare" during the times of the judges may have been that few individuals made themselves unreservedly available to God. The Lord may have been waiting for just such a man as Samuel, who would serve Him faithfully with a whole heart.

5. HE RAN TO ELI: There is poignancy in this picture of a youthful Samuel running to his master, thinking it was Eli who called him. Samuel's quick response and humble attitude demonstrate he had a true servant's spirit, for he was willing to leap out of bed in the darkest hours of the night to answer the call of his master.

6. THE LORD CALLED YET AGAIN: In this passage we gain some insight into the character of God as well. The Lord is not an overbearing master who is quick to punish a servant who does not respond perfectly to His call. He recognized Samuel's willing spirit and continued to call him even though Samuel misunderstood.

7. SAMUEL DID NOT YET KNOW THE LORD: This statement explains why Samuel was confused, for he had never heard the voice of the Lord before and therefore did not recognize it. Yet it is also a searing indictment against Eli, who had failed to lead his young protégé into a personal knowledge of God. Eli, as the high priest, was accountable to teach Israel about God and demonstrate in his own life what it meant to walk with the Lord. But he had failed to do so.

8. THEN ELI PERCEIVED: Eli's failure to teach others about God was probably a result of his own failure to walk closely with Him. He was slow to recognize God's call of Samuel because he had grown unfamiliar with His voice. This was a mistake Samuel would not repeat in his life.

SAMUEL'S FIRST PROPHECY: The Lord comes to Samuel and stands patiently, waiting for him to listen. Then He gives him his first word of prophecy.

10. THE LORD CAME AND STOOD AND CALLED: Here we gain another insight into the unfathomable grace of God. Notice He did three things here: He came; He stood; He called. The almighty God, Creator of heaven and earth, humbled Himself to come into the presence of His servant—something no earthly king would ever do. What is more amazing is that He stood there, patiently waiting for His servant to recognize His presence—again, a reversal of earthly roles toward one's sovereign. Finally, He patiently called to Samuel, gently urging him to understand the God whom he served. The additional statement that He did this "as at other times" underscores the fact that the Lord is gentle and patient with all His children. He humbles Himself to the role of a servant in order to bring a fuller understanding of Himself to mankind.

11. I WILL DO SOMETHING IN ISRAEL: Here Samuel received his first prophecy from the Lord, and it proved to be one of his most difficult messages to deliver. Yet the Lord was giving Samuel this prophecy for the express purpose that he should tell it to others. This is always the Lord's goal when He gives His people a revelation: we are not to keep the word of the Lord to ourselves but to proclaim it to others.

12. ALL THAT I HAVE SPOKEN CONCERNING HIS HOUSE: The Lord had already sent another unnamed prophet to Eli to pronounce judgment on him and his family (see 1 Samuel 2:27–36). One might ask why Eli was held accountable for the sins of his children, but we must remember he was the high priest. Those who teach God's people are held to a higher level of accountability. Eli had failed to teach the people about the God they worshiped, and the Lord held him responsible for permitting immorality in His temple.

13. HE DID NOT RESTRAIN THEM: It is worth noting that Eli did, in fact, confront his sons about their wicked behavior (see 1 Samuel 2:22–25). His words were stern, but there are times when words are not enough. Eli's sons were serving at the temple, acting as priests and intermediaries for God's people, and were subject to a high level of accountability. Eli's simple scolding was thus grossly insufficient in dealing with their crimes. He should have removed his sons from their priestly office and replaced them with men whose hearts were turned fully to the Lord. When he didn't do that, the Lord

stepped in and did it for him—replacing both of the sons, and Eli himself, with Samuel.

14. THE INIQUITY OF ELI'S HOUSE SHALL NOT BE ATONED FOR: Numbers 15:30–31 states that "the person who does anything presumptuously . . . brings reproach on the LORD, and he shall be cut off from among his people. Because he has despised the word of the LORD, and has broken His commandment, that person shall be completely cut off; his guilt shall be upon him." The phrase translated *presumptuously* literally means "with a high hand"; that is, with disdain for the will of God. When Eli failed to fulfill his priestly duties by removing his wicked sons from office, he brought that curse on his own head as well.

DELIVERING BAD NEWS: Samuel discovers that being the Lord's spokesman can involve some heavy responsibilities—including bringing bad news to people he loves.

15. SAMUEL WAS AFRAID TO TELL ELI THE VISION: Here is another poignant glimpse into Samuel's character. He loved his master and was loath to bring him such bad news. Yet this is part of a prophet's responsibility: he must tell others the message God has given, whether that message is good news or bad. Many Christians today shy away from telling others the truth about God's coming judgment, and some go so far as to deny there is an eternal punishment awaiting those who reject Christ. But the gospel contains both good news (that eternal life is freely available to all who believe) and bad news (that those who reject Christ will spend eternity in hell). We do a gross disservice when we try to water down the Word of God.

17. GOD DO SO TO YOU: Eli recognized a prophet risked God's anger if he did not deliver the Lord's complete message. Christians do well to keep this in mind—we are commissioned to proclaim the full gospel of Christ, not just the parts that seem pleasing to the culture around us.

19. LET NONE OF HIS WORDS FALL TO THE GROUND: This phrase contains a double meaning. On one hand, it means Samuel's prophecies were all fulfilled by the Lord, which proved he was a true prophet of God. On the other hand, it means Samuel never failed to deliver God's message to His people. He recognized his high calling as the Lord's spokesman to Israel and treated God's word with care and respect.

20. SAMUEL HAD BEEN ESTABLISHED AS A PROPHET OF THE LORD: The people of Israel knew Samuel was speaking the word of God because his prophecies all came to pass (see Deuteronomy 18:22). That same test should be applied today to those who claim to speak the word of God. If their message does not coincide with the clear teachings of Scripture, it means they are not speaking a message from God.

UNLEASHING THE TEXT

1) If you had been in Samuel's place, how would you have reacted to hearing your name called in the middle of the night?

_____

_____

_____

2) Why did the Lord come to Samuel and stand before him? Why did the Lord call Samuel multiple times? What does this reveal about God's nature and His desire to save?

_____

_____

_____

3) How could Samuel have lived in the temple his entire life and yet still not know God? What does this reveal about a true saving knowledge of God?

_____

_____

_____

4) Why did the Lord send such a devastating judgment on Eli? What had he done wrong?

_____

_____

_____

_____

EXPLORING THE MEANING

We are called to deliver God's Word faithfully—even when it seems unpleasant. Samuel provides a glaring contrast to Eli, the high priest. Eli was responsible to ensure that the worship of the Lord was carried out according to God's commandments, yet his own sons were guilty of gross misconduct and sexual immorality. Their sins were leading others into sin, and the Lord's name was being profaned in Israel. Yet Eli did little to stop them, and by his failure he brought God's wrath on himself and his whole family.

Samuel, on the other hand, was always faithful to carry out the Lord's instructions, and he was willing to deliver bad news when the Lord commanded. He had spent his entire childhood in the temple, serving alongside Eli, and he loved the high priest as a father. Yet his first assignment as a young prophet was to deliver horrible tidings to Eli—a heavy responsibility for a teenager who had never before uttered a prophetic word. Nevertheless, he understood the weight of his calling and faithfully told Eli the heartbreaking news.

In a similar way, we are called to be a faithful testimony to the world around us and teach others the Word of God. Our calling is similar to Samuel's in that we are God's witnesses in the world—and we must take care to deliver His Word accurately. The world does not want to hear that eternal judgment awaits those who reject Christ—for that matter, the world often gets angry when Christians teach Jesus is the only way to salvation. But these messages are an integral part of the gospel, unpopular though they may be, and God's people need to be faithful in proclaiming the full message of what God has said.

Those who teach God's Word are called to a higher standard of accountability. The Lord pronounced a harsh curse on the family of Eli, declaring that none of his descendants would live to old age. At first glance it seems almost unfair that God would punish Eli for the sins of his sons, to say nothing of carrying that punishment into future generations. But God is never unjust, and the very severity of the sentence forces us to recognize that the Lord took Eli's failure very seriously.

Eli was complicit in the sins of his sons because they were more important in his eyes than God (see 1 Samuel 2:29). He did this by permitting them to carry on their vile behavior in the temple even though it disgraced the name of the Lord, thereby demonstrating he cared less about God's honor than about his sons' pleasure. He had an obligation as a father to care for his sons, and he had an obligation as the high priest to care for the things of the Lord—and both those obligations required him to firmly discipline his sons for their sins.

This principle specifically holds true for those who are in spiritual leadership. James warns us, "Let not many of you become teachers, knowing that we shall receive a stricter judgment" (3:1). Yet it is also true in a more general sense for all Christians. Those who bear the name of Christ are called to display His character to the world around them and are to refrain from many of the pastimes and habits in which their neighbors indulge.

The Lord is pleased by a willing heart. Samuel was scarcely more than a boy, certainly no older than fourteen, when he heard a voice in the deep watches of the night calling his name. He leaped out of bed without complaining and rushed to his master—only to find Eli had not called him. When he heard the voice a second time, he did not lie in bed and ignore it; he ran once again to Eli's side. When the Lord gave him some bad news for Eli, his heart quaked at the thought of delivering such a message to the man who was like a father to him, yet he did so in obedience to the Lord—and he delivered it in full.

Eli, on the other hand, served the Lord less willingly. When he was faced with the unpleasant task of disciplining his sons, he did not obey fully but only halfheartedly. Samuel's quick and willing obedience, even in unpleasant tasks, stood as a tacit rebuke to the high priest. We will see the same contrast later in these studies between Saul and David.

The Lord does not want His people to serve Him grudgingly, but willingly and cheerfully. Jesus said, "Take My yoke upon you and learn from Me, for I am gentle and lowly in heart, and you will find rest for your souls. For My yoke is easy and My burden is light" (Matthew 11:29–30). And 2 Chronicles 16:9 tells us that "the eyes of the LORD run to and fro throughout the whole earth, to show Himself strong on behalf of those whose heart is loyal to Him."

REFLECTING ON THE TEXT

5) Why was Samuel afraid to tell Eli what the Lord had said? What would you have done in Samuel's situation?

_____

_____

_____

6) What does it mean that Samuel let none of God's words "fall to the ground"? What does that reveal about Samuel's character? About your responsibility to God's Word?

_____

_____

_____

7) Why was Eli's failure so grievous in God's eyes? What does this teach about spiritual accountability?

_____

_____

_____

8) Why did the Lord instruct Samuel to deliver a message to Eli that the priest had already heard? What did Samuel gain from this? What effect did it have on Eli?

_____

_____

_____

PERSONAL RESPONSE

9) Do you have a willing heart toward God? Or do you obey Him out of a sense of compulsion? Explain.

_____

_____

_____

10) In what ways have you answered the Lord's call in your own life? In what ways have you come to a saving knowledge of Him?

_____

_____

_____

3

THE ARK IS CAPTURED

1 Samuel 4:1–6:21

DRAWING NEAR

What are some things people try to do to "secure" the Lord's favor when they make a request? What is the problem in thinking they can actually do this?

_____

_____

_____

THE CONTEXT

In the previous study, we saw how God called out to Samuel in the middle of the night and gave him a difficult first assignment: to deliver bad news to Eli about God's judgment on him and his family. As this study begins, Eli is still the high priest, and his two wicked sons—Hophni and Phinehas—are still acting as priests under his authority. Time has passed, and Eli is now an old man nearing the end of his life. He has been serving in the temple for forty years.

At the time, the tabernacle for the Israelites was located in Shiloh, and the ark of the covenant was also kept there. The ark symbolized the presence and power of the Lord, yet it seems the Israelites had begun to treat it like a good-luck charm that would ensure them victory over their enemies. In this, we see they had begun to confuse the *symbol* of God's presence with His *actual* presence. In so doing, their understanding of God resembled that of their main enemy, the Philistines.

In this study, we will look at what happened when the people made the rash decision to remove the ark from the temple and take it with them into battle. We will follow the story of the ark as it moves into enemy territory and witness what happens as a result. We will also examine the sad end of Eli's life and the lives of his two sons, whose wicked behavior reflected his own tragic failures. We will see how the message of Eli's life is that doing the "right things" and being in the "right places" does not guarantee a person is right with God—and that the Lord is more concerned with us being obedient to Him than with our outward displays of service.

KEYS TO THE TEXT

Read 1 Samuel 4:1–6:21, noting the key words and phrases indicated below.

> THE FRUIT OF ELI'S SIN: *The Lord's judgment falls on Eli and his sons as prophesied, but the results are more far-reaching still, as Israel loses the ark of the covenant.*

4:1. BATTLE AGAINST THE PHILISTINES: From the period of the judges through the end of David's reign, the Philistines ("Sea Peoples") were an ever-present enemy of Israel.

APHEK: This site is located near the source of the Yarkon River at the southern end of the coastal plain of Sharon, approximately five miles east of the Mediterranean Sea.

3. LET US BRING THE ARK OF THE COVENANT: The people of Israel understood that the Lord was the One who fought their battles and that a defeat indicated something was wrong in their relationship with Him. What they did not understand, however, was that the ark was not a magical good-luck charm that would carry the presence of God wherever they chose. Their confusion underscores the fact that Eli had failed to teach them the ways of the Lord.

5. ALL ISRAEL SHOUTED: This is a sad picture because the people of Israel thought they were placing their trust in the Lord's presence when in fact they

were merely trusting in a manmade object. It shows the Israelites would have been willing to follow the ways of the Lord if only the priests had led them correctly.

7. THE PHILISTINES WERE AFRAID: This could have been a glorious day of victory for the Israelites if they had been truly following the Lord's leadership. Instead, it turned into a day of disgrace, bringing scorn on the name of the Lord because of Eli's poor shepherding.

GOD HAS COME INTO THE CAMP: To the Philistines, an idol was thought to be the actual dwelling place of the deity. Thus, when Israel brought the ark into the camp, the Philistines concluded God was present—an exclamation that reflected their knowledge of God's power.

8. THE GODS WHO STRUCK THE EGYPTIANS: Evidently, the news of God's victory over the Egyptians was common knowledge to the Philistines.

9. SERVANTS OF THE HEBREWS, AS THEY HAVE BEEN TO YOU: Israel's failure to uproot all the inhabitants of Canaan caused them to fall under the judgment of God. As a consequence of this judgment, Israel was enslaved to Philistine oppression (see Judges 10; 13–16). Here, the Philistines feared they would become servants of the Hebrews.

LOSS AND DEFEAT: God soon shows the Israelites the depth of their misunderstanding when He allows the Philistines to capture the ark—the very symbol of His presence.

11. THE ARK OF GOD WAS CAPTURED. In spite of the peoples' hopes to manipulate God, they were defeated, and the ark fell into the hands of the enemy. The view held by both the Israelites and the Philistines that *possessing* the ark was equivalent to having *control* over God will be set in stark contrast with the power and providence of God in the remaining narrative.

HOPHNI AND PHINEHAS, DIED: In fulfillment of the prophecies given in 1 Samuel 2:34 and 3:12, Eli's sons died together.

13. HIS HEART TREMBLED FOR THE ARK: The concern Eli expressed for the ark in this verse is much different from his earlier actions of honoring his two sons over the Lord.

18. HIS NECK WAS BROKEN: As was the case with Hophni and Phinehas, Eli died. Thus, in fulfillment of the word of the Lord, all the priestly line through Eli was wiped out.

HE HAD JUDGED ISRAEL FORTY YEARS: What a tragic end to a life of service! Yet Eli's service was more to himself than to the Lord, and his sons had taken that attitude to its logical conclusion by completely despising the things of God. Eli's life demonstrates a person can be outwardly involved in the service of God while truly being more concerned with service to self.

21. THE GLORY HAS DEPARTED: The word *departed* carries the idea of having gone into exile. Thus, to the people of Israel, the capture of the ark was a symbol that God had gone into exile.

IN ENEMY HANDS: The action now shifts to the Philistines as they move the ark through their territories—and suffer God's judgment as a result.

5:1. ASHDOD: One of the five chief Philistine cities, three miles inland from the coast, and approximately thirty-three miles west of Jerusalem.

2. DAGON: Ancient literature identifies this deity as a fish god, whose image had the lower body of a fish and the upper body of a man. Dagon seems to have been the leader of the Philistine pantheon and is noted to be the father of Baal. Placing the ark in the temple of Dagon was supposed to be a sign of Dagon's power and Yahweh's inferiority—a visual representation that the god of the Philistines was victorious over the God of the Hebrews.

3. FALLEN ON ITS FACE: Ironically, God Himself overturned the supposed supremacy of Dagon by causing the false god to fall over, as if paying homage to the Lord.

4. ITS HANDS WERE BROKEN OFF ON THE THRESHOLD: God's second display of power—the cutting off of Dagon's head and hands—was a common sign that the enemy was dead. It was to be understood as God's divine judgment against Dagon.

5. TREAD ON THE THRESHOLD: Over time a superstition developed among the Philistines that the threshold of the temple was cursed because the head and hands of Dagon had fallen on it. For this reason, the Philistines would not tread on it.

6. THE HAND OF THE LORD WAS HEAVY: In contrast to the hands of Dagon being cut off, symbolizing his helplessness against the power of God, the Lord was pictured to be actively involved in judging the Philistines.

TUMORS: It has been suggested this word refers to the sores or boils caused by an epidemic of the bubonic plague carried by rats. The spread of the disease and its deadly effect make this a likely view.

8. LORDS OF THE PHILISTINES: The men who ruled the chief Philistine cities as kings.

GATH: Another main Philistine city, located twelve miles east of Ashdod.

10. EKRON: Ekron was six miles north of Gath and the closest major Philistine city to Israel's border. The Philistines sent the ark there to see if God was behind their calamity.

THEY HAVE BROUGHT THE ARK . . . TO KILL US: The cry of the Ekronites was an admission that God was the source of their troubles. It is curious the Philistines knew of God's power to strike the Egyptians (see 4:8), yet they believed themselves stronger than Egypt. The severity of the plagues grew increasingly worse, which corresponds to the Philistines' failure to humble themselves before God. Their actions were similar to those of the Egyptians (see Exodus 5–14).

SENDING THE ARK AWAY: The Philistines finally decide enough is enough and send the dreaded object of their destruction back to the Israelites.

6:2. THE PRIESTS AND THE DIVINERS: The Philistines summoned these men, specifically identified in Scripture as having notable fame (see Isaiah 2:6), to figure out how to appease God and stop the plague. The Philistines finally understood they had offended God, and the diviners decided to appease His wrath by sending the ark back to Israel.

3. TRESPASS OFFERING: The purpose behind this offering was for the Philistines to both acknowledge and compensate for their trespass of dishonoring the God of Israel.

4. FIVE GOLDEN TUMORS AND FIVE GOLDEN RATS: It was Philistine custom to make models of their sores (and the rats that brought the plague) in hopes the deity would recognize they knew why he was angry and remove the evil that had fallen on them. The number *five* represents each of the Philistine cities and lords affected by God's judgment.

5. GIVE GLORY TO THE GOD OF ISRAEL . . . HE WILL LIGHTEN HIS HAND: This statement affirms the intention behind the offerings: they were to

halt the dishonor, confess the peoples' sin, and acknowledge that it was God they had offended and that He was the supreme deity.

6. WHY THEN DO YOU HARDEN YOUR HEARTS: The diviners correlate the Philistines' actions of not recognizing the God of Israel with those of Pharaoh and the Egyptians.

7. NEVER BEEN YOKED: The diviners devised a plan to reveal without a doubt whether the God of Israel was behind all their troubles. Using cows that had "never been yoked" meant using animals that were untrained to pull a cart and probably would not go anywhere.

TAKE THEIR CALVES HOME, AWAY FROM THEM: The second element in the diviners' plan was to use nursing cows taken away from their calves. If the cows unnaturally headed off in the opposite direction from their calves, it would indicate their judgment was supernatural.

9. BETH SHEMESH: This was a Levitical city located about fifteen miles west of Jerusalem in the Sorek Valley. It had originally been designated for the descendants of Aaron (see Joshua 21:16). The name means "house of the sun."

THE ARK RETURNS HOME: *The story of the ark's capture concludes with its return to the people of Israel. The people will quickly discover that the same rules regarding its treatment apply to them.*

12. LOWING AS THEY WENT: The cows moaned from instinctive unwillingness to leave their calves behind but went straight to Beth Shemesh, not turning to the right or left. For the Philistines, the inescapable conclusion was that God had indeed judged them.

13. REAPING THEIR WHEAT HARVEST: Sometime in June. The whole city participated in accomplishing these harvests.

14. BURNT OFFERING: Because the cows and cart were used for sacred purposes, they could not be used for everyday purposes. Therefore, the men of Beth Shemesh sacrificed the cows and used the cart for the fire.

15. LEVITES: The men of Beth Shemesh, being Levites, were qualified to move the ark.

16. FIVE LORDS OF THE PHILISTINES: The lords of the Philistines, after seeing the ark had arrived safely, returned to Ekron.

19. LOOKED INTO THE ARK: This action on the part of the men of Beth Shemesh constituted the sin of presumption (see Numbers 4:18–20).

FIFTY THOUSAND AND SEVENTY MEN: Some debate whether this figure is too large. However, retaining the larger number is more consistent with the context of "a great slaughter" and the reference to thirty thousand in 1 Samuel 4:10. However, a scribal error could have occurred, in which case the number would omit the fifty thousand and likely be seventy, as in Josephus.

20. WHO IS ABLE TO STAND: This question is the climax of the narrative of the ark. No one is able to stand against God's judgment. This applied to the people outside the covenant as well as those under the covenant. Presumption before God is unacceptable.

21. KIRJATH JEARIM: A city located approximately ten miles northeast of Beth Shemesh. It would remain the resting place of the ark until David brought it to Jerusalem. This location had long been associated with Baal worship.

UNLEASHING THE TEXT

1) How could a priest of the Lord not know the Lord? What were the consequences of Eli's failure to lead the people, both for his own family and the nation?

_____

_____

_____

2) What was wrong with the Israelites' idea of bringing the ark into battle? What misunderstanding did it show they had about God?

_____

_____

_____

3) Why did the Philistines bring the ark of the covenant into the temple of Dagon? What did they learn about the God of Israel as a result?

_____

_____

_____

4) What are some of the parallels between the plague that afflicted the Philistines in this story and the plagues that afflicted the Egyptians during the exodus?

_____

_____

_____

EXPLORING THE MEANING

Our sin can lead others into sin. The wicked deeds of Eli's sons were bad enough in themselves and more than sufficient to disqualify them for their roles as priests. However, the more damaging aspect to their sins lay in the fact that they also led others into sin. They seduced women at the temple who had come there to serve the Lord, thereby turning their good intentions into wicked deeds.

Eli's failure to teach his sons about the ways of the Lord enabled them to treat God's Word with contempt. On a larger scale, his own disregard for God's Word led the *entire nation* into error. The people of Israel came to think they could control the presence and power of God by using the ark of the covenant as a lucky charm, and this led to the terrible tragedy of losing the ark to the Philistines.

None of us lives in a vacuum. Our decisions and actions always affect those around us. This principle applies to godliness as well as to sin, for just as we can influence others for good by obeying God's Word, we can influence others for evil by disregarding His Word. We must guard against the attitude that some "small indulgence" will not harm anyone, for our actions have consequences we cannot predict.

True religion is not seen in outward symbols. The Israelites, or at least a great number of them, seemed to think the ark possessed special powers. In some way, it seems, they thought the Lord *resided* inside the ark of the covenant. They assumed God lived in a box, and that if they brought that box into battle, they would have success. When they lost not only the battle but also the ark, Eli died of shock, and the people acted as if they had lost their God.

The Lord used this event to punish His people for their sin, to show Eli's ignorance of His true nature, and even to bring a testimony of the greatness of the Lord over the Philistines' god, Dagon. He proved how ridiculous it was for the people to think He resided in a box (or any other religious symbol) and that by losing that symbol, His power was likewise lost. This thinking made the Lord dependent on His people rather than the other way around.

The Lord also demonstrated that He operates sovereignly in our world and is under the control of no one. The Israelites thought they could manipulate God into giving them victory over the Philistines by bringing the ark into battle. However, the Lord showed He was not confined to a symbol and that *He*—not the people—determined the outcome of all things.

Serving the Lord requires obedience to His Word. We see this principle at work in the life of Eli, who served the Lord at the temple in Shiloh for forty years and even acted as one of Israel's last judges. He had risen to the highest level in the priestly class and achieved the greatest honor and responsibility a Levite could obtain. Yet in the end it was all in vain, and he died literally as a broken man.

This principle was also at work in the lives of the men of Beth Shemesh. The Philistines' mistreatment of the ark, the holy symbol of the Lord, brought devastation on them as long as it was in their hands. We would expect to see something different when the ark was returned to God's people, but when the men committed the sin of presumption, they were struck down just as the Philistines had been.

The men's question, "Who is able to stand before this holy LORD God?" (1 Samuel 6:20), emphasizes this point. The Lord required obedience to His

Word, and that applied to both those who were inside and outside His covenant. Knowing God is not an intellectual exercise but a spiritual devotion that comes from submitting ourselves to Him as Savior and obeying Him as Lord. Eli and the men of Beth Shemesh did not live in obedience to God's Word, and we must take care to not repeat their mistake.

REFLECTING ON THE TEXT

5) What were the Israelites' motives when they brought the ark into battle with them? In what ways do people tend to treat God this same way today?

_____

_____

_____

_____

6) When the people of Israel lost the ark, it was symbolic to them of God going into exile. How do the events in this story show this was not the case?

_____

_____

_____

_____

7) Why did the Lord bring judgment against the men of Beth Shemesh? What does this reveal to us about whom He requires to be obedient to His Word?

_____

_____

_____

_____

8) How can the loss of the ark of the covenant and the judgment against the men of Beth Shemesh be traced back to Eli's failure as high priest? What does this demonstrate about the wide-ranging effects of sin?

_____

_____

_____

PERSONAL RESPONSE

9) What effect is your life having on people around you? Are you leading others toward godliness or toward sinfulness?

_____

_____

_____

10) Is there an aspect of God's Word you tend to ignore? What area of obedience might He be calling you toward in the coming week?

_____

_____

_____

4

THE LAST JUDGE
1 Samuel 7:1–17

DRAWING NEAR

Who are some people you know who have been faithful to the Lord throughout their lives? What do you think enabled those people to so faithfully serve God?

_____

_____

_____

THE CONTEXT

Previously, we saw that God had called Samuel to be a prophet in Israel, but He also called him to serve as a judge. The judges were individuals whom God called into leadership over specific segments of Israel, usually over a few of the twelve tribes. The Lord raised them up for the purpose of leading His people into obedience and overthrowing some external foe that was oppressing Israel. Unfortunately, many of these judges were not good examples of godly behavior. Samson, for example, indulged in many forms of disobedience to the Lord's commands, including sexual depravity.

Samuel's leadership marked the end of the judges' period and the beginning of the monarchy. Just as he was faithful in his role of prophet, he was also faithful in his role as Israel's last judge. He led the people to repent of their idolatrous practices, and they gained a great military triumph over their enemies under his guidance. But more important, Samuel demonstrated godliness in his own life and walked in obedience to the Lord's commands. The example he set was one of the most powerful aspects of his leadership as Israel's last judge.

We met the Philistines in our previous study. They were a powerful military force in the land, and their armies were well trained and equipped with the most advanced weaponry. Up to now, their oppression of Israel had been relatively peaceful, but in this chapter we will see them rise up to enforce their rule with an iron hand. What is most interesting is that it was while the Israelites were gathered publicly to repent of their idolatry that the Philistines were motivated to attack them.

Keys to the Text

Read 1 Samuel 7:1–17, noting the key words and phrases indicated below.

ISRAEL LAMENTS: The Israelites have been polluting their worship with pagan practices. Under Samuel's guidance, they now turn their hearts back to God.

7:1. TOOK THE ARK OF THE LORD: As we discussed in the previous study, the ark represented the presence of God among His people. The Israelites had carried it into battle against the Philistines when Eli was still high priest, and it had been captured and carried off to Ashdod, one of the Philistines' five major cities. It had later been taken back into Israel and was being kept at Kirjath Jearim (northwest of the Salt Sea; see the map in the Introduction).

2. IT WAS THERE TWENTY YEARS: That is, the ark had remained in Kirjath Jearim for two full decades by the time Samuel called the assembly at Mizpah (see verse 5). The ark would actually remain in Kirjath Jearim for approximately one hundred years, until David carried it back as one of the first acts of his kingship (see 2 Samuel 6).

ALL THE HOUSE OF ISRAEL LAMENTED AFTER THE LORD: During the period of the judges, the people of Israel had fallen into a cycle of sin and repentance. They would turn away from obedience to the Lord, and He would permit an enemy to oppress them. After a period of suffering, the people would cry out to God for help, and He would raise up a leader to serve as judge and deliverer. Under the spiritual leadership of Eli, the nation had again turned to the pagan practices of the world around them, and the Lord had removed His hand of blessing. Under Samuel's direction, however, the nation was beginning to lament the loss of their special relationship with God.

3. PUT AWAY THE FOREIGN GODS: The people of Israel had added many elements of pagan religion into their worship practices, and the Lord used numerous judges to purify His people. Israel had not utterly abandoned the law of Moses or stopped worshiping the Lord at His temple, but they had adulterated their worship practices with other practices from the Canaanites. The church today is in danger of this same failure as it becomes fascinated with worldly entertainment and fixated with secular concepts of success rather than sticking closely to the Word of God. The Lord will not permit His people to create their own syncretistic religion, selecting at a whim this idea or that practice from the world's abundance of false gods. He calls His people today to "serve Him only," just as He called Israel in Samuel's time.

4. THE BAALS AND THE ASHTORETHS: Baal was a male pagan god, and Ashtoreth was female. Both were viewed by the Canaanites as holding authority over crops, fertility, and military strength. They were represented in pagan temples by statues, and Canaanite worship practices included temple prostitution and other immoral rites. The Israelites had probably incorporated both the idols and the wicked practices into their worship of God. As already noted, the Lord does not permit His people to invent their own approaches to worship, even if some worldly practices seem "culturally relevant."

SAMUEL GATHERS THE PEOPLE: Samuel takes spiritual leadership in Israel, calling the people together for collective repentance before the Lord.

5. MIZPAH: Located about eight miles southwest of Bethel. It became one of the cities of Samuel's circuit.

I WILL PRAY TO THE LORD FOR YOU: Samuel demonstrated one of the important responsibilities of a prophet by interceding on behalf of others. Interestingly, there is no record of any of the previous judges offering to pray for the people.

6. DREW WATER, AND POURED IT OUT BEFORE THE LORD: Pouring out water before the Lord signified repentance (see Lamentations 2:19).

WE HAVE SINNED AGAINST THE LORD: Samuel's act of pouring out the water and the people's acknowledgment of its significance reveal that true repentance had taken place. The condition of the heart superseded the importance or righteousness of the ritual.

SAMUEL JUDGED THE CHILDREN OF ISRAEL: Samuel would represent the transitional figure in Israel's form of government from various judges to a single king. The role of judge included leading the people in warfare and settling domestic disputes. Samuel, however, was also a prophet who was given specific revelations from the Lord, which he communicated to the people throughout his lifetime. As we will see, his role as both high priest and prophet included acting as a counselor and advisor to the future king.

THE PHILISTINES MAKE WAR: The Philistines fear Samuel is organizing a revolt against them and gather their armies to squash any rebellion.

7. THE LORDS OF THE PHILISTINES WENT UP AGAINST ISRAEL: The Philistines discovered the people of Israel had gathered at Mizpah and feared Samuel was leading Israel to rebel against their rule. But the Lord's time for that overthrow had not yet come; He was more concerned that His people cleanse their lives of paganism. God would indeed overthrow the Philistine rule, but first the people needed to repent and return to Him. The Lord ultimately used David to completely defeat the Philistines, while Samuel's role was to turn back the hearts of the people.

THEY WERE AFRAID OF THE PHILISTINES: From a human perspective, the Israelites had good reason to fear. The Philistines were a powerful and wealthy nation, possessing five major fortified cities, each with a well-trained standing army. Their weapons were technologically advanced, while Israel's were rather primitive. Yet the people of Israel had not learned an important lesson in their relationship with God: the Lord would be faithful to fight their battles. He had defeated many overwhelming foes in the past, including the elite forces of Egypt, and they could depend on Him to do the same in the future.

8. DO NOT CEASE TO CRY OUT TO THE LORD OUR GOD: Here we see the Israelites had indeed repented of their paganism and had turned their hearts back to the Lord, referring to Him as "our God." They had also learned the important lesson that they could not use the ark of the covenant—or any other material object—as some sort of talisman to invoke the power of God at their whim. The Lord would indeed defend Israel, but He wanted His people to approach Him in prayer and obedience.

THE LORD FIGHTS THE BATTLE: As He has done countless times in the past, the Lord sends a powerful miracle to defeat Israel's foes. Samuel sets up a monument to remember the event.

10. THUNDERED WITH A LOUD THUNDER: The Lord used a variety of spectacular methods to beat Israel's foes. On one occasion, He caused the sun to stand still (or the earth to stop in its rotation; see Joshua 10). At other times, He rained down great hailstones or even fire from heaven. In numerous other confrontations, the Israelites did not even need to go into battle. On this occasion, He evidently sent some tremendous natural phenomenon, such as a terrific thunderstorm or perhaps an earthquake. The Philistines were stunned and confused, which allowed the army of Israel to win a great victory. The Lord had shown once again that He was the one to fight for His people, and the victory was entirely His.

11. BETH CAR: The location is unknown.

12. EBENEZER: Literally "stone of help." Previously, Joshua had instructed the people to build a pile of stones beside the Jordan River to remind them of the Lord's miracle in parting the river for them to cross on dry land (see Joshua 4). Samuel was now continuing the practice by setting up monuments to commemorate this great victory that the Lord had won for His people. It is important to be reminded frequently of all God has done for us, lest we forget and begin to distrust His faithfulness. This is the reason Jesus instituted the Lord's Supper (see Luke 22:19).

THUS FAR THE LORD HAS HELPED US: This does not mean, "Well, God has helped us so far—let's hope He'll continue to do so." On the contrary, it means the Lord had been faithful to Israel throughout the past, and the people could depend on His continued help in the future. Samuel was teaching the Israelites they could trust fully in the faithfulness of the Lord. The stone memorial would serve as a constant reminder of that fact.

13. THE PHILISTINES WERE SUBDUED: The Lord gave Israel the victory over the Philistines, discontinuing their threat for the immediate future during Samuel's judgeship. However, while the Philistines were subdued, they were not utterly overcome. They did not attack Israel again during Samuel's lifetime, but they did resume their oppression during the kingship of Saul.

ALL THE DAYS OF SAMUEL: Just as this section opened in verse 1 with Samuel being pictured as God's agent, so here the section closes with the Lord working powerfully all throughout the days of Samuel.

14. EKRON TO GATH: These two locations, mentioned earlier as chief Philistine cities, became the eastern border of the Philistines. The territory to the east of these cities was freed from Philistine control and returned to Israel.

AMORITES: Whereas the Philistines resided in the coastal plains, the Amorites resided in the hills west of Israel between the Jordan Valley and the coastal plain. As with the Philistines, the nation of Israel was at peace with this foreign nation.

A CIRCUIT: The circuit was an annual trip that Samuel made across the land. He would travel to Bethel, Gilgal, Mizpah, and then return once again to Ramah. This allowed him to manage the affairs of all the people.

RAMAH: The first major division of the book (1 Samuel 1:1–7:17) ends with Samuel returning to Ramah to judge the people.

UNLEASHING THE TEXT

1) In what ways had the people of Israel become unfaithful to the Lord? What things needed to be purified in their lives?

_____

_____

_____

2) What circumstances and people did the Lord use to bring Israel to repentance? What was involved in their repentance?

_____

_____

_____

3) How did the Lord demonstrate His faithfulness to Israel in this story? What did He require the Israelites to do?

_____

_____

_____

4) How did Samuel exercise his roles as both a judge and prophet of Israel? What are some of the ways in which he remained faithful to this dual calling?

_____

_____

_____

EXPLORING THE MEANING

The Lord gives victory in the battle. The Philistines were a commanding nation, and their armies were feared throughout Canaan. The Israelites were armed with slings and bows at best, and many fought with simple farm tools. They were no match for the iron weapons and chariots of the mighty Philistines, and their hearts were filled with fear when the enemy gathered in force on their borders.

But their powerful foe could not stand before the wrath of God! He sent them into confusion simply by roaring out with a thunderous voice. The Israelites still had to participate in the battle on that occasion, just as the Lord still involves His people in spiritual warfare today, but ultimately the victory belonged to Him alone. God's people continue to face many foes today, whether from the open hostility of the world or from spiritual attacks of Satan. Yet the same principle applies: the Lord will defend and protect His people, and He can never lose.

It is important to remember what God has done for us in the past, most notably in the sacrifice of His own Son on the cross at Calvary. As the apostle Paul rhetorically asked, "If God is for us, who can be against us? He who did not spare His own Son, but delivered Him up for us all, how shall He not with Him also freely give us all things?" (Romans 8:31–32).

The spiritual battle begins at home. The Lord brought a tremendous victory against the Philistines, but not before His people repented of their pagan practices. The Israelites had been guilty of adulterating their worship with idolatry and immorality. As a result, they had been severely routed in battle against the Philistines—even to the point of losing the precious ark of the covenant.

The Lord had removed His hand of blessing from His people because they were being unfaithful to Him. The same principle applies today. The Lord is always faithful to His people, but He expects His people also to be faithful to Him. He calls us to be obedient to the teachings of Scripture and keep our lives pure from sin.

This does not mean God expects us to never fail, "for He knows our frame; He remembers that we are dust" (Psalm 103:14). It does mean, however, that we are to be quick to confess any sin and that our lives should be growing in the image of Christ. God's concern for our practical holiness begins on the home front, as He calls us to purify our lives and walk in obedience to Him.

True leaders are examples in godliness. God appointed both Samuel and Eli to lead His people—Eli as high priest, Samuel as a judge and prophet—but their effects on the nation were vastly different. Eli permitted his sons to act as priests under his authority despite the fact they were severely corrupt. He apparently did nothing to lead the nation as a whole out of idolatry and back to faithful obedience. During the time he was high priest, the Philistines captured the ark of the covenant—the symbol of God's presence.

Samuel, on the other hand, did not hesitate to confront the people with their idolatry. He led the nation out of their pagan practices and back to obedience to the Lord's commands. He also interceded on behalf of the Lord's people and established an annual circuit so he could travel throughout Israel and manage the affairs of the people. God used his faithfulness to bring great blessing on Israel.

Samuel did more than just judge the people of Israel—he also gave them a clear example of godliness through his life. True spiritual leadership is seen in those who are examples of godliness. Praying for others, obeying the Word of God, and confessing sins are the marks of true spiritual leadership.

REFLECTING ON THE TEXT

5) What worldly philosophies and practices have been embraced in Christian circles today? Which, if any, of these have you allowed into your own life?

_____

_____

_____

_____

6) Why didn't the Lord simply defeat the Philistines miraculously without any fighting on the part of the Israelites? What does this suggest about your own spiritual battles?

_____

_____

_____

_____

7) In what ways does Samuel provide an example of godly leadership? Of godly obedience?

_____

_____

_____

8) Why did Samuel set up the memorial of Ebenezer? What purpose did it serve for the people of Israel? For Israel's neighbors?

_____

_____

_____

Personal Response

9) Are there areas in your life in which you need to confess and repent? Spend time asking the Lord to show you anything that is not pleasing to Him.

_____

_____

_____

10) What "Ebenezers" do you have to remind you of God's faithfulness? What kinds of memorials can you set up as future reminders?

_____

_____

_____

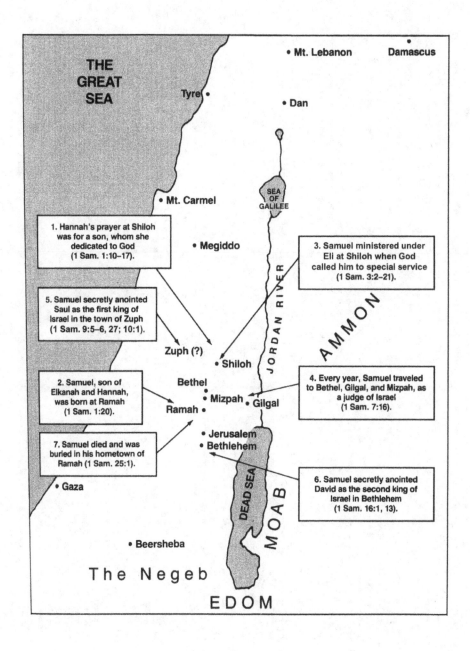

THE
GREAT
SEA

• Mt. Lebanon   Damascus

Tyre •

• Dan

• Mt. Carmel

SEA
OF
GALILEE

• Megiddo

1. Hannah's prayer at Shiloh
was for a son, whom she
dedicated to God
(1 Sam. 1:10–17).

3. Samuel ministered under
Eli at Shiloh when God
called him to special service
(1 Sam. 3:2–21).

JORDAN RIVER

5. Samuel secretly anointed
Saul as the first king of
Israel in the town of Zuph
(1 Sam. 9:5–6, 27; 10:1).

AMMON

Zuph (?)

• Shiloh

Bethel

2. Samuel, son of
Elkanah and Hannah,
was born at Ramah
(1 Sam. 1:20).

• Mizpah
Ramah •   • Gilgal

4. Every year, Samuel traveled
to Bethel, Gilgal, and Mizpah, as
a judge of Israel
(1 Sam. 7:16).

7. Samuel died and was
buried in his hometown of
Ramah (1 Sam. 25:1).

• Jerusalem
• Bethlehem

6. Samuel secretly anointed
David as the second king of
Israel in Bethlehem
(1 Sam. 16:1, 13).

• Gaza

DEAD SEA

MOAB

• Beersheba

The Negeb

EDOM

5

THE PEOPLE DEMAND A KING
1 Samuel 8:1–22

DRAWING NEAR

What are some of the ways people demand things from God? Why do you think God sometimes answers these demands though He is obviously under no obligation to do so?

_____

_____

_____

THE CONTEXT

In the previous study, we saw how Samuel served as a judge to the people and led them to a great military triumph over their enemies. As time passed, he continued to faithfully act as both judge and prophet in Israel. He literally devoted his entire life to serving Israel, and that service was not always easy. At this point, one might expect that he would be treated with respect and honor. But that was not the case.

Part of the problem was that Samuel's sons were repeating the same pattern as Eli's sons: abusing their power and living in wickedness. However, there was also a bigger problem: the people of Israel had focused their eyes on their influential neighbors, and they were beginning to imitate men rather than God. Finally, the elders of Israel decided to come to Samuel and demand he replace himself with a king. The people wanted to be ruled by a monarchy rather than by judges.

The Lord, of course, was not caught off guard by this demand. He had already established plans for the future monarchy in Israel. But, as we will see, the impetus for this change of government was the desires of the people, not the best system established by God. The Lord knew a kingship would bring servitude to the people, and He knew they would not be happy with their choice. Sometimes it isn't good to get our heart's desires.

Keys to the Text

Read 1 Samuel 8:1–22, noting the key words and phrases indicated below.

Samuel's Sons: Samuel is now an elderly man, and his sons have families of their own. He has appointed them as judges, but they are not walking with the Lord.

8:1. when Samuel was old: Samuel was probably in his sixties at this point (c. 1043 BC).

he made his sons judges over Israel: This was an unusual thing to do. For approximately 350 years, the Lord Himself had selected individuals to serve as His judges, and they did not choose their successors. We will discover, however, that Samuel's weak spot was indulging his own sons—a failing he shared with Eli, with similar results.

2. Beersheba: Located approximately forty-eight miles south of Jerusalem. This location had been important to Abraham and Isaac, who both dug wells there (see Genesis 21; 26).

3. his sons did not walk in his ways: This is an interesting statement. One would expect that Samuel's sons did not walk in the *Lord's* ways, rather than in Samuel's ways. It might possibly suggest that Samuel, like Eli, had failed to fully instruct his sons in the ways of the Lord. It is important to live a life that demonstrates godliness to one's children, but that lifestyle must also be accompanied with clear instruction in God's Word. An example

without instruction will lead the children to imitate the parent, but we are called to imitate Christ.

THEY TURNED ASIDE AFTER DISHONEST GAIN: Eli's sons were members of the priesthood, while Samuel's sons were judges, or political leaders. They did not serve at the temple, yet the effect of their corruption was similar. The Lord showed grace to Samuel's family by removing the sons from power in a gentle way rather than by the type of tragedy that Eli's family suffered.

CALLING A MEETING: *The elders of Israel come to Samuel and demand he do something about the future of Israel's leadership. They want a king.*

4. THE ELDERS OF ISRAEL GATHERED TOGETHER: The elders' request for a king was not wrong in itself. In fact, the Lord had provided instruction for this event hundreds of years earlier (see Deuteronomy 17:14–15). It is worthy of note, however, that the Lord had fully anticipated both the request for a king and the motives behind that request. The elders' request was not wrong, but their motives were.

5. YOU ARE OLD: This reason for demanding a king was somewhat dubious. It is reasonable to recognize that God's prophet was getting old and that his death might be imminent. (It wasn't, as it turned out.) But it is God's responsibility to raise up prophets and leaders for His people. Samuel may have been getting old, but the elders needed to trust that the Lord would appoint a successor in His own time.

YOUR SONS DO NOT WALK IN YOUR WAYS: This complaint was entirely valid. Samuel had made a mistake in this transaction by appointing his own successors and naming his sons as judges. Just as the elders were not free to select God's anointed, so also Samuel—God's anointed at the time—was not free to choose his successors.

LIKE ALL THE NATIONS: This was the foundational reason for the elders' demand of a king: they wanted to be like the pagan nations around them. The people of Israel had struggled for generations to become like the world around them, and that struggle had led them again and again into idolatry and immorality. Even in Saul, their first king, their desire to be like the world would lead to an unstable and ungodly kingship.

Samuel Feels Rejected: Samuel is not pleased by the elders' demand for a king. The Lord is not pleased either, for they have actually rejected Him.

6. THE THING DISPLEASED SAMUEL: Samuel was disappointed, at least in part, because he felt the people were rejecting him. He had spent his life serving God's people, first as a boy in the temple and then later as the nation's judge and the Lord's prophet. He may also have sensed the greater danger behind the request for a king: the people wanted a human leader they could see rather than the Lord whom they could not see.

SAMUEL PRAYED TO THE LORD: Once again, we get a glimpse into the godly character of this man. When the people and circumstances went against him, he did not lash out or retaliate but turned to the Lord for help. He demonstrated the attitude the Lord desired in all His people: trust in Him to fight their battles and guide them.

7. THEY HAVE REJECTED ME: God's plan was for Him to be His people's King and for them to trust Him fully for their needs and safety. But the people of Israel were perpetually lured away from God's plan by the ways of the world. The church today faces this same danger. It is easier for us, according to our human mindset, to trust our future to human beings whom we can see, but this demonstrates a lack of trust in the faithfulness and power of God.

8. ALL THE WORKS WHICH THEY HAVE DONE: The nation of Israel had repeatedly seen the power of God acting in astonishing miracles on their behalf, yet they had repeatedly refused to trust Him. What was worse, they accused the Lord of being evil, claiming again and again that He had led them out of their Egyptian slavery simply to destroy them in the wilderness or at the hands of some powerful foe. Once the Lord had settled them safely in Canaan—just as He had promised—they turned their hearts away from Him and embraced false gods and immoral pagan practices. The truly amazing aspect of this wretched cycle is the fact the Lord continued to extend His grace to a nation that was so quick to reject Him as Lord.

SO THEY ARE DOING TO YOU ALSO: People who reject God's sovereignty and lordship will also reject those who serve Him. Moses faced this same situation as the people of Israel repeatedly tried to remove him from leadership. Those who stand boldly for obedience to God's Word will often experience the hatred of the world.

GIVE THEM WHAT THEY DEMAND: *The Lord instructs Samuel to heed the demands of the people and give them a king. But He also warns Israel they will not like it.*

9. HEED THEIR VOICE: This is a sobering principle: the Lord will eventually give us the things we continually clamor for, even if those things will prove harmful to us. He does not do this out of a vindictive spirit, for He will warn us and attempt to steer us in a course that will bring blessing and godly character. However, if we persist in demanding our own way, we run the terrible risk that the Lord will grant us what we demand.

10. SAMUEL TOLD ALL THE WORDS OF THE LORD: Samuel's life was characterized by his faithfulness to God's word. The Lord, in turn, "let none of [Samuel's] words fall to the ground" (1 Samuel 3:19).

11. HE WILL TAKE YOUR SONS: Israel had never had a standing army before the time of the kings. This set the nation apart from the world around them, particularly the Philistines, who kept a well-trained military ready for battle at all times. From a human perspective, it must have made the Israelites feel vulnerable to have no organized military force prepared to meet a foe on the battlefield, but from the Lord's perspective, there was no need for a standing army. It was never Israel's army that defeated her foes; it was always the Lord's mighty arm.

12. SOME TO PLOW HIS GROUND AND REAP HIS HARVEST: Israel had never experienced a centralized government before, and there had never been official "civil service." Again, this was contrary to the world around them, whose city-states included large, full-time staffs that were employed by their kings. This might have sounded attractive to the Israelites at the time, but they did not realize such employment made them vassals to their king rather than free and self-sufficient farmers and shepherds.

HIS WEAPONS OF WAR AND EQUIPMENT FOR HIS CHARIOTS: The people commonly went into battle with short bows, slings, scythes, and other primitive weapons. They faced enemies who boasted iron swords, heavy shields, and terrifying chariots, yet they would still be victorious. Once again, the arsenal of God's people is not manmade; it is the power of God fighting on their behalf. "For we do not wrestle against flesh and blood, but against principalities, against powers, against the rulers of the darkness of this age, against spiritual hosts of wickedness in the heavenly places" (Ephesians 6:12).

14. HE WILL TAKE THE BEST OF YOUR FIELDS: Land ownership in Israel was passed on from generation to generation as part of a family's inheritance. It was not generally bought and sold the way real estate changes hands in modern America but was kept in the family as a sacred possession. It was a great violation of the Lord's intended system of land ownership to have a king seize one's lands for his own use.

15. A TENTH OF YOUR GRAIN AND YOUR VINTAGE: Having no centralized government also meant the Israelites had never before paid taxes. Their entire financial obligation had been to the Lord and His temple. The "tenth" was a tithe, the percentage a person would give to the temple or to the priests for their service. Samuel's point was that if the people added a king, they would have an additional tithe to pay as well.

17. YOU WILL BE HIS SERVANTS: Samuel was warning the people that a centralized human government under a human king would compete with the Lord's position in their culture. The king would demand to be the people's sovereign, but only God Himself was sovereign. The king would exercise authority over every aspect of their lives—land, income, crops, livestock, even the people themselves. Central human government was not the Lord's original design for society, because the larger it grew, the more it would set itself in God's place.

18. YOU HAVE CHOSEN FOR YOURSELVES: Here again we see the principle that the Lord does permit His people to bring suffering on themselves if they persistently demand it.

20. THAT OUR KING MAY JUDGE US AND GO OUT BEFORE US AND FIGHT OUR BATTLES: As we have seen repeatedly, these were aspects of the Lord's role in the nation of Israel. The people were indeed rejecting the Lord by demanding to have a mortal lead and defend them. The more people depend on human government, the less they depend on the Lord.

UNLEASHING THE TEXT

1) Why did the Israelites want a king? Why were they unsatisfied with judges?

_____

_____

_____

2) What part did Samuel's sons play in Israel's desire for a king? What part was played by their envy of the surrounding nations?

_____

_____

_____

3) Why was Samuel disappointed by the elders' request for a king? How would you have responded in his situation?

_____

_____

_____

4) How would a monarchy change the lives of the Israelites? What were they gaining? What were they losing?

_____

_____

_____

EXPLORING THE MEANING

It is dangerous to insist on having our own way. Throughout the Israelites' exodus from Egypt, they continually fought against the leadership of Moses. They panicked at every obstacle and frequently accused God of having evil intentions toward them. When Moses went up the mountain to speak with God face to face, the people built a golden idol and began to worship it. They did not want to do things God's way; they wanted to do things their own way.

The Lord raised up many judges to lead the people once they were settled in the Promised Land, but this was not what the people wanted. They preferred the lifestyle of their pagan neighbors and even embraced pagan deities and immoral religious practices. Eventually, the Lord acquiesced to their demands for a king, but He did so with dire warnings of the servitude that would come along with a monarchy. Yet still the people insisted.

God's ways may not seem as easy or attractive as the world's ways, but they are always for our best interests. It is always the best course to obey the written Word of God, even if that course may seem costly at the time. In the long run, living life God's way is the best way.

Even sinful decisions fit into God's sovereign plan. The Lord is not the author of sin, nor does He tempt His children. But God's children can sometimes be so self-willed and stubborn that He permits them to have their demands—even when those desires lead to suffering. However, as this passage shows, God had made provision in the law of Moses for the day when Israel would have a king. He had even anticipated their sinful motives for doing so (see Deuteronomy 17:14).

Beyond this, the kingly line God was about to establish would eventually lead to the Messiah, Jesus Himself. This is a clear example of people's sinful motives and decisions being part of God's perfect plan, which He uses to redeem those very people.

We are to follow God, not imitate the world. The nation of Israel was surrounded by pagan nations, many of whom were wealthy and powerful. It would have been easy for them to look at their Philistine neighbors and envy their prosperity and military power, and easier still to become tempted by the carnal practices seen in their pagan temples. The people may even have justified such envy with the attitude that if the Philistines prospered by serving Baal, it couldn't be all that bad!

In order to imitate another person, we have to pay close attention to that person. In order to imitate the Canaanites, the Israelites had to focus their eyes on their neighbors, which meant taking their eyes *off* their God. What we focus on becomes our role model. If we immerse ourselves in the entertainments and lifestyles of the world, we will end up imitating the world.

Christians are to immerse themselves in the Word of God, regular corporate worship, and prayer. When we fill our hearts and minds with the presence and Word of God, our eyes will be steadfastly focused on Christ—and we will find ourselves imitating Him. As Paul wrote, "Be imitators of God as dear children. And walk in love, as Christ also has loved us and given Himself for us, an offering and a sacrifice to God for a sweet-smelling aroma" (Ephesians 5:1–2).

Those who reject Christ will also reject His followers. Samuel was deeply grieved when the elders of Israel demanded a king. He had devoted his life to serving them and serving the Lord, and he must have thought the people were being ungrateful. He probably felt like a failure, as though his life of faithful service had been in vain.

This is a common situation for those in spiritual leadership. One may give freely and sacrificially to others, striving to obey God's Word while humbly serving in the most menial tasks, and then find people are not satisfied. At that point, the godly servant may wonder whether his or her self-sacrifice has been in vain.

But as the Lord gently reminded Samuel, those who reject Him will also reject His servants—and that principle is still true today. We are called, like Samuel, to serve the Lord faithfully and fully and leave the consequences in His hands. There will be times of blessing and times of suffering, but those who suffer in the Lord's service share in the highest calling of all: the sufferings of Christ. "Share . . . in the sufferings for the gospel according to the power of God, who has saved us and called us with a holy calling" (2 Timothy 1:8–9).

REFLECTING ON THE TEXT

5) In your opinion, why did Samuel repeat the mistake Eli had made by appointing his disobedient sons to leadership? What can we learn from their mistakes?

_____

_____

_____

_____

6) How did Samuel respond to the elders' request for a king? How does his response compare with your own response in similar situations?

_____

_____

_____

7) Why did the Lord allow Israel to have a king, even though He knew it would bring suffering to them? How does the Lord take our own sins and sovereignly use them as part of His perfect plan?

_____

_____

_____

8) Why did the Israelites want to imitate their neighbors, even after seeing the futility of serving pagan idols? What leads a person to imitate others?

_____

_____

_____

PERSONAL RESPONSE

9) Are you content to live as God directs, or do you tend to want things your own way? What areas in your life might the Lord want you to submit to Him?

_____

_____

_____

10) Who or what do you tend to imitate in your life? What do you need to do this week to imitate Christ more closely?

_____

_____

_____

6

SAUL COMES TO POWER

1 Samuel 9:1–10:27

DRAWING NEAR

How would you describe the difference between humility and a lack of self-esteem?

_____

_____

_____

THE CONTEXT

So it was the people had demanded a king, and the Lord had agreed to their demands. The young man the Lord would select for the job was named Saul. He was strong and tall, standing head and shoulders above his peers. He was from a wealthy and influential Benjamite family and was probably among the better-educated class in his land. His family had many servants, so he was familiar with being in a position of authority.

From the world's perspective, Saul had the perfect background and ideal qualifications for a king. But the world's perspective is not God's perspective. Saul may have appeared kingly on the outside, but as we will see, his heart was not turned toward the Lord, which was the primary qualification for Israel's king. His life would ultimately demonstrate a failing common in politics even today: doing what is expedient while always looking out for one's own interests.

However, at the beginning of Saul's story he seemed to be a young man of great promise. When we first meet him, he is dutifully going about the important task of recovering some lost donkeys for his father. He is certainly not expecting to be named Israel's first king, nor is he eager to accept the role—as demonstrated by the fact that he hides among the supplies when the proclamation is made that he will be king.

On one hand, this suggests a great humility in Saul, as though he felt unworthy and unequipped for the role. He was "little in his own eyes," as Samuel would later note (1 Samuel 15:17). In this, his view of himself was accurate. But on the other hand, his actions show that even from the start he did not see the world through God's eyes. The Lord saw him as a man of greatness, fit to become the sort of king that He desired. Unlike David, Saul did not recognize the Lord would give him the strength to perform what He had commanded him to do.

KEYS TO THE TEXT

Read 1 Samuel 9:1–10:27, noting the key words and phrases indicated below.

> *INTRODUCING YOUNG SAUL: We meet Saul when he is a young man, just prior to being anointed as Israel's first king. He has great potential, both for good and for failure.*

9:1. A MIGHTY MAN OF POWER: Saul's father was a wealthy and influential man, and Saul was likely raised with all the advantages the world had to offer. From the world's perspective, he would have had everything needed to become a great king. The Lord's perspective, however, is vastly different from that of the world.

2. A CHOICE AND HANDSOME SON: There are some interesting similarities and contrasts between the backgrounds of Saul and David. Both men were described as handsome, though Saul was also very tall, literally standing head and shoulders above his peers. Emphasis was generally placed on the external appearances of leaders.

SAUL: The name *Saul* means "asked for." Saul was the king the people had asked for, and he lived up to all of Samuel's dire warnings. The Lord would later select David to rule, and he would prove to be the sort of king of God's own choosing.

3. THE DONKEYS . . . WERE LOST: Lost donkeys meant lost wealth. Saul's father, Kish, had servants who could have gone looking, but he chose Saul to oversee this important task.

4. SHALISHA . . . SHAALIM: The locations are geographically unknown.

5. LET US RETURN: Saul would frequently give up following the Lord's commands when circumstances became difficult. This is one way in which Saul differed from David. While Saul gave up on his assignment without completing it, David would fight both a lion and a bear singlehanded to serve his father and protect his sheep.

SEEKING THE LORD'S PROPHET: Saul's servant informs him that a "seer" lives nearby and suggests they go seek him out. The "seer," however, has more than donkeys in mind.

6. THERE IS IN THIS CITY A MAN OF GOD: It would appear that Saul's ignorance of the ways of God extended to his earliest years. He needed his servant to tell him that Samuel, God's prophet and judge, lived in this city. The entire nation of Israel was aware of Samuel and where he lived, so it was not a good sign that Saul didn't even know who he was.

7. WHAT SHALL WE BRING THE MAN: In those days, it was common to offer a gift to a prophet if one were asking for guidance. The gift expressed gratitude and thankfulness for the service of the man of God. In this we see that Saul was concerned with outward appearances and doing the socially correct thing, but not so concerned with doing what was right in God's eyes. He was careful to obey social etiquette in offering a gift, but would not be so careful to obey what the prophet commanded him.

8. ONE-FOURTH OF A SHEKEL OF SILVER: This represented about one-tenth of an ounce. Saul did not even provide his own gift for Samuel—though he was the son of a wealthy man—but instead relied on his servant's generosity. Even from his earliest appearances we find Saul was not a strong leader; he followed the leadership of his servants.

9. A PROPHET WAS FORMERLY CALLED A SEER: A *seer* was so named because of his God-given ability to know or see the future. By the time the book of 1 Samuel was written, that person had become known as a *prophet,* which is why the author needed to include this note.

12. HIGH PLACE: This was Canaanite in background (see Deuteronomy 12:2–5). Before the temple was built, the priests used high places for sacrifice because they provided the best vantage point for the participants.

13. HE MUST BLESS THE SACRIFICE: The man of God offered the sacrifice to the Lord as an act of worship.

14. THERE WAS SAMUEL: This passage once again demonstrates the absolute sovereignty of God over the affairs of men, even the mundane affairs of daily life. The Lord used some wandering donkeys to lead Saul to Samuel in order to anoint him as king. Each step along the way could be viewed as simple coincidence, but there are no coincidences in God's eyes.

16. ANOINT HIM: This represents a "setting apart" for service to the Lord.

COMMANDER OVER MY PEOPLE: The word *commander* literally means "one given prominence" or "one placed in front." The title referred to one who was designated to rule.

THEIR CRY HAS COME TO ME: The people had been crying out for deliverance from the Philistines, their longtime rivals, just as they had done for liberation from the Egyptians.

LITTLE IN HIS OWN EYES: Saul is taken aback by Samuel's words of greeting. He thinks himself unfit to be king. But Samuel knows different, for he has heard from God on the matter.

17. THIS ONE SHALL REIGN OVER MY PEOPLE: God identified Saul to Samuel to assure there was no mistaking whom He was choosing to be king.

18. WHERE IS THE SEER'S HOUSE: A reference to Samuel's house.

20. ALL THE DESIRE OF ISRAEL: Saul was to become the focus of the Israelites' hopes for military victories over their enemies.

21. WHY THEN DO YOU SPEAK LIKE THIS TO ME: At this time in his life, Saul was still small in his own eyes. Yet the seeds of his prideful stubbornness were already sown, even at this early date.

22. THE HALL: The place where those who were invited ate with Samuel after the offering of the sacrifice at the high place.

SIT IN THE PLACE OF HONOR: Saul was anointed publicly and with great celebration. He was seated in the place of honor among thirty guests and was fed the choicest parts of meat.

24. THE THIGH . . . SET APART FOR YOU: Samuel received the thigh, the portion of the sacrifice reserved for the priest (see Leviticus 7:32–34). Giving this choice piece of meat to Saul reflected his new status as the designated king.

SAUL IS ANOINTED: Samuel now privately anoints Saul to be king over Israel and prophesies that the Spirit of the Lord will come on him. These events soon come to pass.

10:1. THE LORD HAS ANOINTED YOU COMMANDER: This private anointing affirmed the Lord had chosen Saul to be the leader of Israel and had set him aside for His service.

2. ZELZAH: Zelzah was probably near Ramah, located between Bethel and Bethlehem, where Rachel died (see Genesis 35:19; 48:7).

3. TABOR: The location is unknown but probably near Bethel.

5. THE PHILISTINE GARRISON: Most likely the garrison in Geba in Benjamin, about five miles north of Jerusalem.

A GROUP OF PROPHETS: Literally "sons of the prophets." They were young men being trained by Samuel for the prophetic ministry.

6. THE SPIRIT OF THE LORD WILL COME UPON YOU: There is a dire contrast between this empowering of the Holy Spirit and the one that came later in Saul's life. On both occasions Saul prophesied among the Lord's prophets, but the later event would accentuate his disgrace rather than his anointing as king (see 1 Samuel 19).

TURNED INTO ANOTHER MAN: Perhaps the saddest part of Saul's story is that it did not need to turn out as it did. The Lord loves to transform people from selfish sinners into selfless saints, and Saul could have become Israel's greatest king. But during his lifetime, he would make a habit of following his own ways rather than the Lord's will.

8. SEVEN DAYS YOU SHALL WAIT: This was one of Samuel's first commands to Saul at the beginning of his kingship. As we will see, it would be the very command he would disobey when he later offered sacrifices to the Lord instead of waiting for Samuel.

9. GOD GAVE HIM ANOTHER HEART: Saul began his kingship with the one thing needed to defend Israel: the empowering of the Holy Spirit. Yet even this did not guarantee he would walk faithfully with the Lord because he did not know God in a saving way.

12. WHO IS THEIR FATHER: This question was asked to find out the identity of the leader of the prophetic band that now included Saul.

16. THE MATTER OF THE KINGDOM: Saul did not tell his uncle the information Samuel gave him about becoming king. This might reflect his humility at the time.

SAUL HIDES IN THE BAGGAGE: Saul's selection as king is now made public to the nation of Israel. However, Saul will again demonstrate his lack of faith in himself by hiding in the baggage.

17. SAMUEL CALLED THE PEOPLE TOGETHER: This took place shortly after Samuel's private anointing of Saul as Israel's first king.

20. BENJAMIN WAS CHOSEN: Saul was probably selected by the casting of lots.

22. HIDDEN AMONG THE EQUIPMENT: Saul knew he was going to be selected as king, but his response was to run away and hide. The Lord saw Saul as a man of greatness, but Saul never learned to see himself that way. As a result, the vision Saul did have of God's plans became less and less accurate over time. He did not believe the Lord would give him the strength to perform what He had commanded him to do.

23. HE WAS TALLER THAN ANY OF THE PEOPLE: Saul's physical stature was impressive. The fact he was head and shoulders above the other people gave him a kingly presence.

25. THE BEHAVIOR OF ROYALTY: Samuel reminded the people of the regulations governing the conduct of kings (see Deuteronomy 17:14–20).

26. WHOSE HEARTS GOD HAD TOUCHED: Saul went back home to Gibeah accompanied by "valiant men" who were eager to affirm God's choice of him as king.

27. BUT SOME REBELS: Literally "sons of Belial." Some of the men did not recognize Saul with the respect befitting a king, and so they "despised him."

UNLEASHING THE TEXT

1) What are some of the traits we see in Saul from this early picture of his life?

_____

_____

_____

2) What characteristics did Saul possess that made him a good choice for king in the people's eyes? How did these differ from God's standards of what made a good king?

_____

_____

_____

3) Why did Saul balk at Samuel's desire to anoint him king? What does this say about the way he viewed himself and the world?

_____

_____

_____

4) How might Saul have become a great king? What are some of the indications we see in this story as to why he ended up going astray?

_____

_____

_____

EXPLORING THE MEANING

If we make a habit of obeying the Lord, it will be easier to obey Him in stress-ful times. Saul was concerned with outward appearances and took great care to say and do the "right things." He fretted about having a suitable gift for the seer when he couldn't find his donkeys. He was concerned about the *etiquette* of dealing with God's prophet but not so concerned about the *obedience* that came with it.

Samuel, in contrast, had made it an overriding habit to obey the Lord's voice. He had learned that lesson as a boy in the temple, and he had continued to practice it the rest of his life. When the Lord later commanded him to anoint David as king, he obeyed in spite of the fact that he was risking his life in the process. Samuel obeyed the Lord in difficult circumstances because it was his habit—a habit that he had developed on a daily basis.

We make something a habit by doing it frequently over an extended pe-riod of time. Physical exercise can become a habit if we do it each day for a few weeks. Obedience to God's Word can also become a habit simply by the routine of obeying on a daily basis.

God resists the proud but gives grace to the humble. When we first meet Saul, we are not presented with a picture of a man who had great faith in his abilities to govern. He was "little" in his own eyes, and yet the Lord said to Samuel, "This one shall reign over My people" (1 Samuel 9:17). As long as Saul main-tained this humble attitude, the Lord was able to work in him and through him to achieve His purposes for Israel.

James writes, "Draw near to God and He will draw near to you . . . Humble yourselves in the sight of the Lord, and He will lift you up" (4:8, 10). Truly humble people submit themselves to God's sovereign authority as ruler of the universe, give their full allegiance to Him, obey His commands, and follow His leadership. They draw near to God by pursuing an intimate relationship with Him and long for communion with Him. They recognize the honor of being in the presence of a majestic and infinitely holy God.

Even though Saul did not see himself at first as a man of greatness, the Lord was able to work through his humble submission and bring him great victory over his enemies. However, when Saul began to view himself as greater than he was, his attitude led him away from humble submission to the Lord's will. As a result, the Lord raised up another man to serve as king in his place. God gives grace to humble followers but not to those who proudly set themselves against His purposes in this world.

It is God who places those who govern us in authority. Saul would not prove to be an effective king. From the start, he did not display the type of courage or faith in God that one would expect to find in the Lord's anointed. As time went along, his grip on sanity would prove to be increasingly tenuous. What's worse, he would become plagued by an evil spirit and subject to demonic attack and oppression. He would act in an unjust manner and become obsessed with keeping power, regardless of the cost to himself or his family.

Nevertheless, Saul *was* the king whom God had anointed over Israel, and all Israel was called to obey him and submit to his authority. Not even David—the one who would become the object of Saul's wrath—was exempt from this injunction. As Paul later wrote, "Let every soul be subject to the governing authorities. For there is no authority except from God, and the authorities that exist are appointed by God. Therefore whoever resists the authority resists the ordinance of God, and those who resist will bring judgment on themselves" (Romans 13:1–2).

The world is not lacking in corrupt leaders and inept politicians, and some Christians are faced with genuine, life-threatening persecution for their faith. But God's Word teaches us that believers are to submit themselves to the authorities the Lord has placed us under—even when those authorities are unjust. "Therefore submit yourselves to every ordinance of man for the Lord's sake, whether to the king as supreme, or to governors, as to those who are sent by him for the punishment of evildoers and for the praise of those who do good" (1 Peter 2:13–14). The only exception to this rule is when an authority commands one to violate the law of God.

REFLECTING ON THE TEXT

5) How did Saul exhibit poor leadership qualities in his interaction with his servant?

_____

_____

_____

6) Read Judges 6:11–18. What similarities do you see between Gideon's responses to God's call and Saul's responses? How did God use them both in spite of their protests?

_____

_____

_____

7) What does it mean that God made Saul "into another man" (1 Samuel 10:6)? What changed in him when the Spirit of the Lord came upon him?

_____

_____

_____

8) Why do you think this didn't ultimately make Saul a good king? What responsibilities did he have in his role as leader of God's people?

_____

_____

_____

PERSONAL RESPONSE

9) Which habit is strongest in your life: the habit of obedience or the habit of indulgence? What area of obedience could you strengthen this week?

_____

_____

_____

10) What gifts has God given you? How are you using those gifts to obey Him more fully? How are you demonstrating faith that God will use those gifts to achieve His purposes?

_____

_____

_____

7

SAUL'S FAILURE AS KING

1 Samuel 13:1–15; 15:1–35

DRAWING NEAR

What are some ways people try to "bargain" with God to get out of doing something they know He wants them to do? What is the end result of such bargaining?

_____

_____

_____

THE CONTEXT

The people had demanded a king, and the Lord had selected one: a young man named Saul from the tribe of Benjamin. As we have seen, he was tall, strong, wealthy, and probably well educated. He had everything going for him from the world's perspective. Furthermore, the Spirit of the Lord had come on him and given him another heart.

As our passage opens, Saul has been king for just two years, and already he has experienced many victories from the Lord. He has successfully rallied the people to defend against a threat from the Ammonites, who were terrorizing the people of Jabesh Gilead. After this great military victory, all the people came to Gilgal to crown Saul as their king and rejoice that the nation had finally been united.

On that great day, Samuel had said, "If you fear the LORD and serve Him and obey His voice, and do not rebel against the commandment of the LORD, then both you and the king who reigns over you will continue following the LORD your God. However, if you do not obey the voice of the LORD, but rebel against the commandment of the LORD, then the hand of the LORD will be against you" (1 Samuel 12:14–15). It would prove to be a telling prophecy.

Saul rides the wave of his success and favor with the people into his next battle against the Philistines. At first things go well, just as they had before against the Ammonites. But the day came when the battle grew fierce, and Saul's army quickly deserted. This would prove to be the big test of his heart. Whom would he serve? Would he be willing to submit himself to the Lord as the true King of Israel? Or would he take that authority upon himself?

This would truly be the moment when Saul would either show he was a man of faith after God's own heart or a man of weakness in pursuit only of his own interests.

KEYS TO THE TEXT

Read 1 Samuel 13:1–15, noting the key words and phrases indicated below.

SAUL MAKES WAR: Saul has experienced success against the Ammonites and is quick to lead the people into open war against the Philistines. In this, he is obeying the Lord's commands.

13:1. SAUL REIGNED ONE YEAR: The original numbers have not been preserved in this text. It literally reads, "Saul was one year old when he became king and ruled two years over Israel." Acts 13:21 states Saul ruled Israel for forty years, but his age at his accession is recorded nowhere in Scripture. Probably the best reconstruction of verses 1–2 is, "Saul was one and (perhaps) thirty years old when he began to reign, and when he had reigned two years over Israel, then Saul chose for himself three thousand men of Israel."

2. MICHMASH . . . BETHEL . . . GIBEAH: These three locations are in the mountainous area just north of Jerusalem.

JONATHAN: His name means "the LORD has given." Saul's firstborn son and heir apparent was evidently old enough to serve as a commander in Israel's army, much like David when he killed Goliath. His first act was to attack a Philistine garrison.

3. GEBA: This was located approximately one mile southwest of Michmash, separated by a deep ravine. The fact the Philistines had a garrison there, near the heart of Israel, indicates the extent of their dominance over the Lord's people.

4. GILGAL: The town of Saul's confirmation as king by Samuel and the people.

5. THIRTY THOUSAND CHARIOTS AND SIX THOUSAND HORSEMEN: This was an immense Philistine fighting force. The chariots and cavalry alone could have easily subdued Israel, whose army did not possess such powerful weapons. In fact, the small army that remained with Saul was armed mostly with farm tools. Only Saul and Jonathan possessed swords, and those swords would have been made of bronze rather than iron.

BETH AVEN: Literally "house of nothingness." It was located less than one mile southwest of Michmash.

7. GAD AND GILEAD: Areas east of the Jordan River.

ALL THE PEOPLE FOLLOWED HIM TREMBLING: The people were in fear over the probable Philistine retaliation.

8. HE WAITED SEVEN DAYS: Samuel had instructed Saul to meet him at Gilgal, where he would join him after seven days (see 1 Samuel 10:8).

SAUL VIOLATES GOD'S LAW: *Things in the Philistine war suddenly take a turn for the worse, and Saul finds himself in dire straits. At this point, his obedience to the Lord vanishes.*

9. HE OFFERED THE BURNT OFFERING: This was expressly forbidden. Only priests were permitted to offer sacrifices, and all priests were from the tribe of Levi. It is true Saul was in a tight corner with his army deserting, but circumstances are never an excuse to ignore God's commands. It is a serious matter for anyone to set aside God's requirements, but it is especially serious for those in spiritual leadership. Even today the Lord has set certain requirements on those who can and cannot act in the capacity of spiritual leadership

(see 1 Timothy 3:1–12; Titus 1:5–9). Christians should not ignore these roles any more than Saul should have violated the priestly code.

10. AS SOON AS HE HAD FINISHED: It is possible Samuel waited the full seven days to test Saul's commitment to the Lord's commandments. Whether or not it was a deliberate test, Saul demonstrated he was more committed to expedience than to obedience.

11. WHEN I SAW: Saul reacted not by faith but based on what he saw. He feared losing his men and did not properly consider what God wanted him to do.

12. I FELT COMPELLED: Saul offered three excuses for his sin: (1) his army was scattering, (2) Samuel's appearance was delayed, and (3) the Philistines were about to attack in overwhelming force. From a human standpoint, Saul merely did what he had to do in a difficult situation. But from God's point of view, difficult circumstances are never an excuse for disobedience.

14. NOW YOUR KINGDOM SHALL NOT CONTINUE: This clearly demonstrates the Lord was testing Saul's heart in this situation. If he had remained steadfast in obeying His commands, he would have demonstrated a heart that was committed to the Lord—and the Lord would have established Saul's lineage on the throne of Israel for all time. Instead, Saul proved his heart was not committed to following God as his sovereign, and the Lord would find another man whose heart was right. That man would be David.

A MAN AFTER HIS OWN HEART: The man after God's own heart is completely committed to following the Word of God.

15. FROM GILGAL TO GIBEAH: This was about a ten-mile trip westward. Samuel left Saul, realizing that Saul's kingship was doomed.

Read 1 Samuel 15:1–35, noting the key words and phrases indicated below.

> GOD'S JUDGMENT ON THE AMALEKITES: *We move forward in time to Saul's battle against the Amalekites, a people group who had attacked the Israelites on their way out of Egypt.*

15:2. HE AMBUSHED HIM: The Amalekites were a wandering tribe descended from Esau, the brother of Jacob. They had attacked Israel without provocation when the people were traveling from Egypt, and the Lord had vowed to wipe them out as a result (see Exodus 17:8–13; Deuteronomy 25:17–19).

3. UTTERLY DESTROY ALL THAT THEY HAVE: There were certain occasions when the Lord commanded His people to "utterly destroy" a city, with all its inhabitants and possessions. Such cities were "set apart" or "dedicated" to God's wrath (see Deuteronomy 13:12–15).

KILL BOTH MAN AND WOMAN: The Lord reserved certain cities for complete destruction when the hearts of their inhabitants had become completely hardened against Him. When those cities were destroyed, the Israelites were strictly forbidden from taking the smallest object in plunder. Absolutely *everything* had to be destroyed—both living beings and inanimate objects—because the Lord had dedicated them to judgment.

4. NUMBERED THEM: Already the Lord's prophecy concerning kings was coming to pass as Saul conscripted several hundred thousand men into his army.

SAUL DISOBEYS GOD'S COMMAND: The Lord has demanded the tribe of Amalekites to be wiped out completely, but Saul only obeys in part.

9. SAUL AND THE PEOPLE SPARED AGAG: Saul committed the same sin as Achan (see Joshua 7) by stealing things that were consecrated to the Lord's judgment. Achan stole only a few articles, but Saul stole on a large scale. What's worse, he led his entire army into sin.

EVERYTHING DESPISED AND WORTHLESS: This demonstrates where Saul's heart truly lay: in serving himself. It is easy to give to the Lord those things that one does not need or care about, but quite another to give Him one's best. It is also sobering to realize that the "despised and worthless" things in Saul's eyes included all the people of Amalek—except the king.

11. IT GRIEVED SAMUEL: Samuel was grieved that Saul had brought the Lord's anger against the Israelites, and he spent the entire night crying out to the Lord on their behalf. This is part of what it means to be a man after God's own heart—to view people and circumstances from the Lord's perspective and share in His deep concern for others.

12. SET UP A MONUMENT FOR HIMSELF: Saul again demonstrated where his true allegiance lay by building a monument to himself rather than to God. This is a stark contrast to Ebenezer, the monument Samuel constructed to remind the people of God's faithfulness (see 1 Samuel 7:12).

13. I HAVE PERFORMED THE COMMANDMENT OF THE LORD: Saul probably believed at the moment that he really had obeyed the Lord's command. After all, hadn't he killed most of the Amalekites? But partial obedience is not obedience at all; it is self-service.

15. THEY HAVE BROUGHT THEM: The moment Saul was confronted with his sin, he instantly blamed someone else—"they have brought them . . . the people spared [them] . . . [but] the rest we have utterly destroyed." This is a hallmark of the self-serving individual, who is quick to seek his or her own advantage and quick to pass the blame.

> GOD REJECTS SAUL: *Saul has shown his heart is turned toward himself rather than toward God. The Lord is about to reject him in favor of a man truly after His own heart.*

17. WHEN YOU WERE LITTLE IN YOUR OWN EYES: Saul had been shy and hesitant to take on the role of king suddenly thrust on him—to the point he had hidden himself in a stack of military equipment on his coronation day. However, he had changed over time as the power he wielded brought out the weaknesses in his character. This is the reason the Lord insists on His people making Christlikeness their first priority. David had developed godly character before becoming king, and that character strengthened his reign.

21. TO SACRIFICE TO THE LORD YOUR GOD: The statement in this verse is terrible in its indictment of Saul. First, he told an outright lie, saying the people had taken the livestock specifically to sacrifice to the Lord when in fact he had taken the plunder for his own gain. Even if they had taken the sheep for sacrifice, that still would not have excused his disobedience. Second, it showed again where Saul's heart stood toward the Lord, for he referred to Him as "the LORD your God" rather than "my God." Saul's god was his own self-will.

22. TO OBEY IS BETTER THAN SACRIFICE: Samuel dismissed Saul's claim that the sheep had been plundered for a burnt offering by cutting to the core of the issue: God wants obedience even more than burnt offerings or costly tithes.

23. REBELLION IS AS THE SIN OF WITCHCRAFT: Saul rebelled against God when he kept what God had told him to destroy. In so doing, what Saul really did, in effect, was reject the lordship of his King and submit himself to the devil. Stubbornness is indeed a form of idolatry, because a stubborn person

makes himself lord of his own life by insisting on having things his own way. The modern focus on self-esteem is merely a contemporary form of this very same idolatry.

HE ALSO HAS REJECTED YOU FROM BEING KING: God rejected Saul fairly early in his kingship, but He did not replace him immediately. Saul reigned a total of forty years.

24. BECAUSE I FEARED THE PEOPLE AND OBEYED THEIR VOICE: Even in the middle of confessing sin, Saul managed to blame other people.

26. YOU HAVE REJECTED THE WORD OF THE LORD: This is a sobering principle that we must not miss: those who persist in rejecting the Word of God will one day be rejected by God. The day of grace will not last forever; now is the time of salvation.

29. HE IS NOT A MAN, THAT HE SHOULD RELENT: This does not mean the Lord is not merciful, for He has promised to remove His hand of judgment from those who repent of sin and turn back to Him. Yet as we've already seen, the time does come when a man has no further opportunities to repent of sin. When that day arrives, the Lord's judgment on the unrepentant sinner is final and everlasting.

30. HONOR ME: In one breath, Saul both confessed he had sinned and asked Samuel to honor him anyway. Once again we see that Saul's heart was fixed on himself rather than on God, for it is God and God alone who shall receive the honor of men. (Notice also, in this verse, Saul's repetition of the phrase "the LORD your God.")

UNLEASHING THE TEXT

1) Why did Saul make a burnt offering to the Lord? Why did Samuel react in anger?

_____

_____

_____

_____

2) If you had been in Saul's place during that fight against the Philistines, what would you have done?

_____

_____

_____

3) Why did Saul not kill the king of the Amalekites? Why did he keep plunder? Why were these things sinful?

_____

_____

_____

4) Why did the Lord demand the complete destruction of the Amalekites, including all their possessions? What does this reveal about the character of God?

_____

_____

_____

Exploring the Meaning

God demands obedience, not expedience. Saul obeyed the Lord's commands as far as they suited his purposes. He attacked the Philistines to throw off their yoke of bondage, which was in obedience to the Lord's will. But when the battle became difficult, he did not hesitate to violate the Lord's commands by usurping the authority of God's chosen priests. He attacked the Amalekites and put them to the sword, but kept the chosen wealth and plunder for himself.

Both of these decisions might be seen as simple expedience. Saul was in a state of emergency with the Philistines surrounding him, and Samuel was nowhere to be found. It was simply expedient for him to offer the sacrifices himself. Defeating the Amalekites was sufficient obedience; slaughtering good sheep would have been wasteful. But in both cases, Saul only obeyed in part, and he felt the freedom to choose for himself exactly *which* part to obey.

The Lord expects His people to obey fully, not in part. Difficult circumstances do not excuse us from obedience to the Lord's commands. The Christian's job is to obey God's Word and leave the consequences in His hands. The Lord had not abandoned Saul when the Philistines surrounded him, and had Saul waited for Samuel, the Lord would have worked a miraculous deliverance for Israel. He has not changed since Saul's time—He will deliver His people from destruction, yet He expects His people to obey His Word.

To obey is better than sacrifice. Saul excused his disobedience by claiming the people had kept the livestock in order to sacrifice them to the Lord. Even if this had been true, it would still have been disobedience to the Lord's explicit command to not take any plunder from the Amalekites.

In the Lord's eyes, obedience is far more valuable than any costly sacrifice or tithe that we might bring before Him. And when we do fall into sin, He wants us to come to Him in repentance and confession rather than with the attitude we can somehow make up for it with good behavior. Both obedience and contrition demonstrate a heart that is turned toward God, and this is more precious in His eyes than any form of sacrifice.

As David would later write, "For You do not desire sacrifice, or else I would give it; You do not delight in burnt offering. The sacrifices of God are a broken spirit, a broken and a contrite heart—these, O God, You will not despise" (Psalm 51:16–17).

Those who persist in rejecting God will one day be rejected by Him. Saul's life was characterized by serving himself rather than God. He frequently obeyed only part of God's commands, setting his own will above God's and effectively viewing himself as equal with Him. By doing this, he was rejecting God's authority in his life.

As we will see in future studies, the day would come when the Lord would no longer offer Saul the opportunity to repent. Saul would speak words of repentance, as he did here when Samuel called out his sin, but we will see that Saul's heart never truly turned away from his sin of self-service. In time, his heart became hardened toward God, and at that point the Lord's grace was unavailable to him.

We are living in the age of grace, when salvation and eternal life are freely available to anyone who will repent and accept God's free gift through Christ. But this day of grace will not last indefinitely. The time is coming—and may be close at hand—when Jesus Himself will return to the earth in judgment. When that day comes, those who have rejected Christ will be cast out of God's presence forever. "Behold, now is the accepted time; behold, now is the day of salvation" (2 Corinthians 6:2).

REFLECTING ON THE TEXT

5) Why did the Lord reject Saul as king? What does this reveal about God's expectations for those in authority over His people?

---

6) In what ways did Saul make expedience more important than obedience? How did his life contrast with Samuel's example?

---

7) If Saul had truly kept the Amalekites' livestock specifically for a sacrifice to the Lord, would that have been acceptable in God's eyes? Why or why not?

---

8) Look at how Samuel dealt with Agag. What lessons can be drawn from that account concerning how believers should deal with compromise and sin in their own lives?

_____

_____

_____

PERSONAL RESPONSE

9) Have you accepted God's gift of salvation? If so, how do you see that in your life? If not, what are you waiting for?

_____

_____

_____

10) Is your life characterized by obedience or by expedience? What area of obedience might the Lord be asking for this coming week?

_____

_____

_____

8

TRANSFER OF POWER
1 Samuel 16:1–23

DRAWING NEAR

What characteristics do we tend to look for in our leaders? In what ways do those qualities match or not match what God looks for in a leader?

_____

_____

_____

THE CONTEXT

The Lord had now rejected Saul as king, and Saul was fully aware that He intended to anoint someone to take his place—someone whose heart was devoted to God. However, by this point Saul did not want to relinquish the throne, which was a strange irony considering he had been reluctant to accept it in the first place. We will see later that Saul's desire to rule was so strong, in fact, that he was willing to kill anyone who attempted to take it from him.

Nevertheless, the Lord called on Samuel to anoint the new king. He was to travel to Bethlehem, where he would find a man named Jesse, and the Lord would point out which of Jesse's seven sons was God's chosen. This was not the first time God had given Samuel a word of prophecy that would prove unpopular, and Samuel understandably feared for his life. In the end, however, he obeyed the Lord and headed for Bethlehem.

David is just a youth when we first meet him, yet he has already developed much godly character. He has been serving his father as a shepherd, a position that involved much hard work and little honor. Yet David has not wasted the assignment but used his lowly position to learn many skills—including the writing of poetry and music.

Those skills were about to become very useful, as the Lord was about to call him from shepherding animals to shepherding His people.

Keys to the Text

Read 1 Samuel 16:1–23, noting the key words and phrases indicated below.

Anointing a New King: The Lord speaks to Samuel and urges him to stop mourning for Saul. He has a new job for him to perform—a new king to anoint.

16:1. How long will you mourn for Saul: This visitation from the Lord probably occurred not long after Saul had been rejected as king. Samuel was mourning Saul's tragedy as one mourns for the dead, recognizing the downfall was final and irrevocable.

Jesse the Bethlehemite: God's new king of Israel (and ultimately the Messiah) would come from the tribe of Judah and from Bethlehem of Judah (see Micah 5:2; Matthew 2:2–6).

I have provided Myself a king: As we saw in a previous study, the Lord chooses for Himself the ones He will anoint. The people had no say in who was to be king, and this time the Lord had chosen a young man whose heart was fully His.

2. If Saul hears it, he will kill me: It is ironic that Samuel's initial reaction to the word of the Lord was fear of Saul instead of rejoicing at God's provision to Israel (and, ultimately, to all the nations). However, later events would show that Samuel's concerns were quite justified. Furthermore, the route from Ramah to Bethlehem would take Samuel through Gibeah of Saul.

I HAVE COME TO SACRIFICE TO THE LORD: The Lord was not instructing Samuel to be deceitful; He was merely adding a new focus to his trip. Samuel was to perform a sacrifice in Bethlehem.

3. ANOINT: Samuel was to perform David's first anointing, symbolizing God's recognition and ordination of him. The following two anointings (in 2 Samuel 2:7 and 5:3) were to establish David as king publicly for the benefit of Judah and Israel.

4. THE ELDERS OF THE TOWN TREMBLED: The entire nation of Israel now knew that the Lord had rejected Saul and that He intended to anoint a new king. Furthermore, the people were already discovering Saul's unstable temperament (which would grow far worse), and they apparently feared a civil war.

DO YOU COME PEACEABLY: The elders, and no doubt all Israel, had also heard of Samuel's execution of Agag (see 1 Samuel 15:33). Israel still closely associated the "seer," or prophet, with the not-so-distant past office of judge.

5. SANCTIFY YOURSELVES: Worship of God was always preceded by cleansing or washing, both of the outward garments and the inner man (see Exodus 19:10, 14; 1 John 1:9).

MEETING THE SONS OF JESSE: Samuel arrives at the home of Jesse and immediately thinks the eldest son is God's chosen. But the Lord does not see as man sees.

6. ELIAB: The firstborn son of Jesse, David's eldest brother. His name means, "My God is Father."

7. DO NOT LOOK AT HIS APPEARANCE: It is quite likely Eliab was a tall, handsome young man, yet Saul had also stood head and shoulders above all the men around him. Even Samuel was susceptible to the tendency to judge truth based on outward appearances, and God had to remind him that He did not choose His anointed because of physical attributes. This was initially a difficult concept for Samuel, as he was accustomed to a king whose only positive attributes were physical.

THE LORD LOOKS AT THE HEART: The Hebrew concept of *heart* embodies emotions, will, intellect, and desires. We tend to believe the evidence of our senses; after all, "seeing is believing." But the fact is that seeing often leads to believing in what is *not* true and viewing things from a worldly perspective rather than God's perspective. The Lord is not impressed with obvious accomplishments, physical appearance, wealth, or any of the things that lead to status in the world. He is only interested in whether a person has a heart devoted to Him.

8. ABINADAB: His name means, "My Father is noble." Samuel, now more sensitive to the leading of God's Spirit, quickly discerned that Abinadab was not God's anointed.

9. SHAMMAH: His name means "Yahweh hears (or heard)."

10. JESSE MADE SEVEN OF HIS SONS PASS BEFORE SAMUEL: With David, Jesse actually had eight sons. The fact 1 Chronicles 2:13–15 indicates Jesse had seven sons must mean one of the eight died afterward.

THE LORD HAS NOT CHOSEN THESE: The firstborn son of the family traditionally had the highest honor. He would receive a double share in the inheritance, and he was viewed as the authority figure in the next generation of the family. It was only natural, therefore, for Jesse to present his sons in descending order. By the time they got to the youngest, they must have been becoming perplexed.

THE RUDDY YOUNG SHEPHERD: Seven of Jesse's sons have been brought before Samuel, and none of them has been chosen by God. There is only one left—the youngest.

11. KEEPING THE SHEEP: The job of shepherd in David's time included a fairly nomadic lifestyle, as the flock was kept moving from one place to another in search of grazing. The shepherd would likely have been the youngest son, or even a hired hand, as it was not considered a position of prominence or honor. On the other hand, Jesse would have honored his eldest son by employing him closer to home.

12. RUDDY: That is, he had a reddish complexion, and perhaps red hair as well. The fact that David's ruddy appearance is mentioned so frequently might indicate he was a redhead, since that was rare among the Israelites in his day. Regardless, David was a handsome young man, yet that was expressly not the reason the Lord chose him. His looks were entirely coincidental to God's selection, for God was looking solely on David's inward appearance.

13. ANOINTED HIM IN THE MIDST OF HIS BROTHERS: David's first anointing is before his family. His second anointing would be before the

assembly of his tribe, Judah. His third anointing would be before the entire nation of Israel.

THE SPIRIT OF THE LORD CAME UPON DAVID: Prior to the death and resurrection of Jesus Christ, God's Holy Spirit did not regularly indwell men and women. The Lord would send His Spirit on someone such as David or the judges to empower them to perform some important task for the protection of Israel. There was no guarantee the Spirit of the Lord would remain on that person for any length of time (hence David's prayer in Psalm 51:11 that the Lord would "take not your Holy Spirit from me"). The Spirit had empowered Saul at one time, but He left him after David's coronation. Christians today, however, have the "seal of the Holy Spirit" as God's guarantee of eternal salvation, and it will never leave or depart.

> GOD SENDS A TROUBLING SPIRIT: *The Spirit of the Lord has come on David, and He has left Saul. Now the Lord goes a step further and permits a demon to trouble Saul.*

14. THE SPIRIT OF THE LORD DEPARTED FROM SAUL: When David's ascent to the throne began, Saul's slow and painful descent also began. Without God's empowering Holy Spirit, Saul was effectively no longer king over Israel, though his physical removal from the throne—and his death—would happen many years later.

A DISTRESSING SPIRIT FROM THE LORD: Numerous theories have been put forward concerning this phrase, including many modern perceptions of various psychological disorders. It is best, however, to take the verse at face value: that the Lord Himself permitted an evil spirit, or demon, to pester Saul. The important thing to recognize here is that the demonic force was completely subject to the will of God, yet it was not the Lord who was torturing Saul. The Lord uses the hatred of Satan and his demons to discipline His people and to punish those who are disobedient, but the Lord will never tempt anyone toward evil.

TROUBLED HIM: Saul's temperament and character were already somewhat volatile. His own inconsistencies grew out of a double mind wanting to serve both God and self. From this time onward, the Lord permitted Saul's instability to gain the upper hand, and he gradually descended into near madness. His severe bouts of depression, anger, and delusion were increased by the evil spirit the Lord had permitted to plague him.

GOD USES DAVID TO HELP SAUL: *Saul's servants quickly recognize their king is being troubled demonically, so they suggest that he find a skilled musician.*

18. I HAVE SEEN A SON OF JESSE: There is nothing here to indicate the person speaking was aware that David had been anointed king. From a human perspective, this suggestion was a mere coincidence. Yet there are no "coincidences" in God's eyes; the Lord deliberately brought David to mind for this job as part of His plan to place him on the throne.

SKILLFUL IN PLAYING: This is an impressive list of David's character qualities. We will later learn he developed his musical skills during idle moments as a shepherd (the book of Psalms bears testimony to his gift as a poet and songwriter). Yet David did not fit the stereotype of a poet, for he was also "a mighty man of valor," having already proven his courage in combat with a bear and a lion (see 1 Samuel 17:36). He was a "man of war," and perhaps most important, also a man "prudent of speech." He knew when to speak and when to hold his tongue, and his conversation was edifying and encouraging.

THE LORD IS WITH HIM: This was the reason David had become so accomplished in so many areas at such a young age. The Lord was with him because he had already demonstrated a heart for God and an eagerness to understand and obey the will of the Lord. When a person builds his life on that attitude, the Lord will produce godly fruit.

19. SEND ME YOUR SON DAVID: Saul did not willingly give up the throne, and his later life would be spent trying to kill God's anointed king. Yet here we see it is impossible to prevent God's will from coming to pass, as Saul invited his own successor into his inner court.

WITH THE SHEEP: David's lowly, humble occupation is emphasized here. He gave evidence of that humility and patience by returning faithfully to his duty following Samuel's anointing.

21. HE LOVED HIM GREATLY: This is a sad passage, for it shows David instantly loved the very king who would one day feverishly and repeatedly try to kill him.

HIS ARMORBEARER: David was most likely one of many such young men assigned to Saul's barracks.

23. THE DISTRESSING SPIRIT WOULD DEPART FROM HIM: Music can certainly have the quality of soothing troubled emotions, and it can also

inflame those who are otherwise calm. But this phrase seems to indicate the Spirit of the Lord was using David and his music to bring genuine spiritual refreshment to Saul, since the "distressing spirit" was of a demonic nature and would not have been subject to Saul's emotions. This shows us once again the mercy of the Lord, for even Saul in his unrepentant state could receive times of spiritual relief through David's service.

UNLEASHING THE TEXT

1) Why was Samuel afraid to travel to Bethlehem and meet Jesse's sons? How did the Lord calm his fears?

_____

_____

_____

_____

2) What qualities did David possess that prepared him to become king? How did those qualities differ from the ones Saul possessed?

_____

_____

_____

3) Why did God's Spirit abandon Saul? Why did He settle on David? What does this reveal about God's priorities in our lives?

_____

_____

_____

4) Why did the Lord send an evil spirit to trouble Saul? What was the Lord trying to accomplish in Saul's life?

_____

_____

_____

_____

EXPLORING THE MEANING

Man looks at the outward appearance, but the Lord looks at the heart. When Saul was anointed king, the qualities the people noticed were that he was tall and strong, standing head and shoulders above his peers. When Samuel met the sons of Jesse, he was immediately taken by the eldest son because he too was tall, strong, and very handsome.

Humans tend to believe the evidence of their senses, which is unavoidable to some extent because we live in a physical world that is experienced through those five senses. But God transcends the things of this material world, and He does not see our lives through five physical senses. God looks on the hearts of people, not on their outward appearances. He sees beyond our actions and accomplishments, weighing our hearts and looking for those who are determined to obey His Word.

It is interesting that the New Testament gives us no physical description of what Jesus looked like—how tall He was or what color His eyes were. The prophet Isaiah even tells us that "He has no form or comeliness; and when we see Him, there is no beauty that we should desire Him" (Isaiah 53:2). The Lord is not interested in such matters; He is concerned with whether we reflect the *heart* of Christ and devote ourselves to obedience and faithfulness. This should be the focus of all God's people.

Even in the midst of discipline, the Lord provides help. Saul had repeatedly rejected the word of God, refusing to obey His commands and preferring to do things his own way. As a result, the Lord had rejected him as king over Israel and had further subjected him to the torments of a demonic influence. Nevertheless, even in the midst of that spiritual suffering, the Lord provided Saul with relief through his servant David.

God's discipline of Saul was intended to bring him into obedience, not to destroy him. Saul had lost the kingship forever, but he could still be brought back into a right relationship with the Lord, which was infinitely more important than whether or not he was king. It is also noteworthy that the Lord used David to provide the relief and encouragement, since David's heart was focused on God and was fully available to the Lord's service.

It is the same with us today. The Lord will send discipline into our lives when we persist in disobedience, but He will also provide assistance. God's purpose for discipline and suffering is to draw us back to Himself when we stray and to make us more like Christ at all times. He will use many tools and methods, including His Word and other people within the family of Christ, but His end ambition is always to make us more like His Son.

Mankind cannot thwart the purposes of God. Saul's kingship was characterized by ignoring the direct commands of the Lord. He obeyed the parts that coincided with his own plans while ignoring anything that did not seem expedient. He had the attitude that he was free to reinterpret the Lord's words to suit his own pleasure, and he did not recognize God's sovereignty as being greater than his own.

Yet Saul himself unwittingly furthered the very plan of God that he was trying to ignore. He would eventually spend all his efforts trying to cling to the throne the Lord had taken away from him, but those efforts were utterly futile. There was simply no way he could prevent or even impede the Lord's will from being carried out.

Saul's attitude is prevalent even today. People often pick and choose what parts of God's Word apply to them—if any—and our culture even teaches that we are sovereign over our own fates. We are encouraged to think that the warnings of Scripture will not apply to our own lives and that we can do as we see fit without any fear of bad consequences. But as the apostle Paul writes, "Do not be deceived, God is not mocked; for whatever a man sows, that he will also reap. For he who sows to his flesh will of the flesh reap corruption, but he who sows to the Spirit will of the Spirit reap everlasting life" (Galatians 6:7–8).

Reflecting on the Text

5) In what ways did Saul inadvertently advance the Lord's plan to anoint a new king? What does this reveal about God's sovereignty?

_____

_____

_____

6) In what ways was Samuel guilty of looking at outward appearances in this story? In what ways did he step out in faith and trust God?

_____

_____

_____

7) Why did God use David's music to drive away the evil spirit when He had permitted the spirit to trouble Saul in the first place?

_____

_____

_____

8) God sent a demonic spirit to Saul, but He also sent relief from that spirit in the form of David's playing. How would you describe God's relationship to evil spirits?

_____

_____

_____

PERSONAL RESPONSE

9) When have outward appearances led you to a wrong conclusion? When have you stepped out in faith, disregarding appearances?

_____

_____

_____

10) What area are you most concerned about in your own life: physical appearance or heart condition? How can you focus more on having a godly heart in the coming week?

_____

_____

_____

9

SLAYING A GIANT
1 Samuel 17:1–51

DRAWING NEAR

How does trusting in God for the small things enable us to trust Him when the big things come? How have you seen this play out in your life?

_____

_____

_____

THE CONTEXT

The battle of David and Goliath is one of the best-known stories in the Bible. Even people who have never read the Bible are familiar with the inexperienced teen who faced the seasoned giant. In fact, the story is often used as a sort of parable by the world to refer to anyone who challenges a stronger adversary. Yet this is not a mere fable but a literal account of an actual historical event, and the people involved were real human beings with real human emotions.

David was just a young man, probably still in his teens, when he faced Goliath. As such he would have experienced all the emotions and aspirations any young man experiences, including fear. He was not a trained soldier and had never worn armor or hefted a shield in his life. The immense giant across the valley, however, was a warrior who wielded superhuman weapons. How could a teenager be expected to charge into battle against such a foe?

We must remember that courage is not the absence of fear but the determination to act in faith in spite of that fear. Conversely, simply rushing forward into a fearful situation is not courage—that is blindness or foolishness. True courage is drawn from the faith that God is sovereign even in the face of adversity. David undoubtedly felt fear as he charged toward that terrible giant, but he kept charging just the same because he knew he was going not in his own strength but in the strength of the Lord.

David recognized God alone is omnipotent and is faithful to fight for His people, just as He had done for him in the past. Thus, while this story of David and Goliath is primarily about God and His glory, it also teaches us lessons about true courage, for we see David's faith tested in an extreme circumstance. But first, we will look at his predecessor's *lack* of courage.

KEYS TO THE TEXT

Read 1 Samuel 17:1–51, noting the key words and phrases indicated below.

> THE PHILISTINES' CHAMPION: *The armies of Israel and Philistia have gathered on opposite sides of a valley. Out of the Philistine ranks emerges a giant who defies the God of Israel.*

17:1. THE PHILISTINES GATHERED THEIR ARMIES: Following the anointing of David and his installation into the court of the king, we are given an update on Israel's situation in regard to its enemies. King Saul was busy with the task that occupied most of his life: fighting the Philistines. On this particular day, the Philistines had gathered in tremendous force to attack Israel, and Saul and his army were filled with fear.

2. VALLEY OF ELAH: The location of the Israelite camp was approximately three miles east of where the Philistine camp was located.

4. A CHAMPION: Literally "the man between two." This is an appropriate appellation, as Goliath stood between the two armies and offered his challenge to a "duel" of hand-to-hand combat. The outcome of this duel would settle the battle for both sides.

SIX CUBITS AND A SPAN: Goliath was nearly ten feet tall! There were other Philistine giants in David's day (archeologists have uncovered numerous giant skeletons), but Goliath was evidently a famed warrior who was idolized by the Philistines and feared by their enemies. A look at his equipment will reveal why.

5. HE HAD A BRONZE HELMET: The ordinary Philistine soldier wore a leather helmet, and most of Israel's fighting men wore no helmets at all, but Goliath's helmet was of bronze.

THE WEIGHT OF THE COAT WAS FIVE THOUSAND SHEKELS: Goliath's coat of mail consisted of metal plates sewn atop a leather jacket and weighed approximately 125 pounds.

6. HE HAD BRONZE ARMOR ON HIS LEGS: Most of the Israelite fighters wore simple hide or leather tunics to protect their chests, and nothing on their lower torso, but Goliath even had metal armor on his legs.

A BRONZE JAVELIN: Most spears and javelins were made of wood, but Goliath's was made of bronze. His spear was so huge it was the size of the wooden beam used to operate a weaver's loom. It was also equipped with an iron spearhead (only the Philistines had iron, which was much harder than bronze), and the head alone weighed some fifteen pounds. Goliath was huge, and his weapons were terrifying.

IN SEARCH OF A MAN: Goliath has issued a challenge to one-on-one combat, but not one man from Israel has stepped forward—including King Saul.

8. CHOOSE A MAN FOR YOURSELVES: Goliath was challenging the Israelites to send out a champion of their own, and the two would fight one on one. This was not uncommon in David's day, as the two champions would decide the outcome of the battle rather than have the two armies engage. The underlying concept was for the two men to be stand-ins not just for their respective armies but also for their respective gods. The result of the combat would reveal the will of the gods—and the relative strength of each deity. Goliath, in effect, was claiming that his god was more powerful than Israel's God.

10. GIVE ME A MAN: The proper man to fight this battle was Saul. He was the king, and therefore he represented the entire nation. He was also the tallest

man in Israel, and was probably the closest physical match to Goliath, though still far removed from the Philistine's stature. Saul, however, was afraid. He did not fulfill his duty as king because he was always looking at outward appearances and focused on his own power. He failed in his courage because he failed in his focus.

11. SAUL AND ALL ISRAEL . . . WERE DISMAYED AND GREATLY AFRAID: Saul and the Israelites had proven that they could be influenced by the fear of men. It is only natural, therefore, that Goliath was their worst nightmare come true.

> DAVID ARRIVES: *Goliath continues to defy Israel's God for forty days, morning and night, without opposition. Then young David arrives on the scene.*

14. DAVID WAS THE YOUNGEST: This fact is important for several reasons. First, we must remember that David was quite young when this battle took place, probably still in his teens. He was also the youngest in his family, which suggests the responsibility for this battle would not fall on his shoulders. If it were up to the sons of Jesse to fight Goliath, it would have fallen to the first-born son to do so. In many ways, David was a ridiculously unlikely opponent for this dreaded giant.

15. DAVID OCCASIONALLY WENT AND RETURNED FROM SAUL: David's duties were divided between his billet with Saul as one of his many armorbearers (see 1 Samuel 16:21) and tending his father's sheep in Bethlehem.

FEED HIS FATHER'S SHEEP: David had not set out that day looking for adventure or hoping to make a name for himself. He was merely doing the work his father had given him to do. God often brings opportunities for service into the lives of those who are focused on doing His work.

16. FORTY DAYS, MORNING AND EVENING: Goliath had been coming forth with his blasphemous defiance against the God of Israel twice a day for more than a month. This situation was a disgrace to Israel's king.

17. EPHAH: About three-quarters of a bushel.

20. THE ARMY WAS GOING OUT TO THE FIGHT: There is a certain irony in this statement, as there was no fight to join. One can picture the Israelite army drawn up across the valley from the Philistines, banging swords against shields, shouting taunts, clamoring for battle—but not fighting. Talk is easy,

but fighting is costly. The Lord's army was indeed looking for a man, just as Goliath had claimed.

23. THE SAME WORDS: On this particular day, Goliath offered the same challenge as he had been giving the past forty mornings and evenings.

24. ALL THE MEN OF ISRAEL . . . FLED FROM HIM: The moment a genuine foe arrived for battle, the bold Israelites melted away in fear. Once again we see the concern for outward appearances minus any concern for genuine obedience. The army, following Saul's example, made a grand display of courage when in fact they had none. They had no courage because they had forgotten the Lord is the one who fights His people's battles.

25. THE KING WILL ENRICH WITH GREAT RICHES: This offer reveals what motivated Saul. David was not motivated by such rewards.

26. TAKES AWAY THE REPROACH FROM ISRAEL: These are David's first recorded words in Scripture, and they reveal both his heart and his motivation. David was concerned that Israel's God was being profaned. It is remarkable that this young man who had never seen military combat was the only one to take umbrage on behalf of God—and he did so the moment he heard Goliath's first blasphemous taunt.

OPPOSITION FROM THE HOME TEAM: David is ready and eager to face the terrible foe across the valley, but first he must face some opposition at home.

28. ELIAB'S ANGER WAS AROUSED AGAINST DAVID: Eliab may have been jealous of his younger brother's preferment by the king, or his conscience may have been smitten that the youngest was proving to be more courageous than he. The end result, however, was that a member of David's own family not only degraded his courage but also, in so doing, tacitly condoned the degradation of the Lord.

32. LET NO MAN'S HEART FAIL BECAUSE OF HIM: Here stood David, a mere teenage shepherd, acting in the role of military leader to the king himself! The king should have been encouraging the army, both by words and deeds, but he had long before failed in that role. Now a man of true courage—a man after God's own heart—was taking over.

35. I WENT OUT AFTER IT AND STRUCK IT, AND DELIVERED THE LAMB FROM ITS MOUTH: Remember the picture of Saul wandering the countryside

in search of his father's donkeys, and then giving up and heading for home? In dramatic contrast, David had risked his own life and limb to save not a whole *flock of donkeys* but just *one sheep*. His great courage was motivated by a deep desire to be faithful to his father's work, and that commitment gave him courage to also face Goliath.

> GOD GIVES THE VICTORY: *David draws his great courage from the Lord. He fully trusts that God will deliver him if he just takes action—and he is not disappointed.*

37. HE WILL DELIVER ME FROM THE HAND OF THIS PHILISTINE: This is the foundation of David's great courage. His courage was in the Lord, not in his own fighting ability. Even if he had not fought the lion or the bear, he would still have come forward to fight against Goliath, for he was fully confident the Lord would honor his obedience and provide the victory.

39. HE HAD NOT TESTED THEM: There was nothing inherently wrong in bearing manmade arms and armor into battle. David would do so himself as he grew to manhood. But his focus was not on the weapons but on his God. He did not know how to use sword and shield, so he was quick to abandon them for the tools with which he was familiar. The weapons made no difference because it was the hand of God that would be wielding them.

42. HE DISDAINED HIM: Those who look only on outer appearances will be quick to despise the people of God, for they cannot see the power of the One who watches over them. Goliath's faith was in his own power and weapons, and David's weapons were laughable by comparison. But Goliath would not be laughing for long.

45. I COME TO YOU IN THE NAME OF THE LORD OF HOSTS: David was fighting for the honor of God's name, which Goliath had defied and slandered day after day. David was absolutely convinced the Lord would honor His commitment to His people, and that is what gave him the courage to step onto the field of battle. The Lord, who rules heaven, would not let Israel be defeated by someone like Goliath, who openly mocked Him.

46. THAT ALL THE EARTH MAY KNOW THAT THERE IS A GOD IN IS-RAEL: Day after day the army of Israel had stood across the valley and shouted similar threats at the Philistines, but David's was quite different. He had come forth to fight for the glory of God and demonstrate to both the Israelites and

the Philistines that the God of Israel was the only true God. He was fighting not for his own glory or the reward of Saul but for the name of God.

UNLEASHING THE TEXT

1) What motivated David to face Goliath? Why was his response to the threat so different from Saul's response?

_____

_____

_____

_____

2) Why did Eliab become angry with David when he expressed interest in fighting Goliath? What does this reveal about Eliab's own motivations?

_____

_____

_____

_____

3) Why did David refuse to take the weapons and armor that Saul wanted to give to him?

_____

_____

_____

_____

4) Why did God allow David to defeat Goliath? What lesson does this teach us about God?

_____

_____

_____

Exploring the Meaning

God receives glory from using those who trust Him. The main point of David's encounter with Goliath is that God can use even the most overmatched person for His glory. David did not win the battle because he had more courage than Goliath. Rather, he won the battle because the Lord was on his side. God could have sent His Spirit to empower Saul as he did in 1 Samuel 10, but then the glory for the victory would have gone to Saul. By using David, the Lord alone received the honor for the victory.

David knew this. While Saul was timid about becoming king, David rushed into battle, trusting the Lord. While Saul continually thought that unless he acted a certain way he would lose his battles, David knew the battle was not his to lose. If David was on God's side, God would get the glory for the victory. Saul spent his life angry because God was not on his side. David spent his life with courage, knowing he was on the side of the Lord. For this reason, the Lord would get the praise because He was the one who achieved the victory.

"Blessed is the man who trusts in the Lord, and whose hope is the Lord. For he shall be like a tree planted by the waters, which spreads out its roots by the river, and will not fear when heat comes" (Jeremiah 17:7–8).

Courage is found by trusting in God's sovereignty. David acted in spite of any feelings of fear he may have had. However, he did *not* simply charge blindly across the valley, hoping things would work out. Blind action in the face of fear is folly, not courage. David was courageous because he knew two things: he would be king over Israel, and the Lord would not be mocked.

Fear grows when we focus our eyes on the things of this world. The Israelite army was terrified because they were busy looking at Goliath and his terrible weapons. David, however, scorned those material weapons. "You come to me with a sword, with a spear, and with a javelin," he said to Goliath. "But I come to you in the name of the LORD of hosts, the God of the armies of Israel" (1 Samuel 17:45). David understood that worldly weapons are powerless against the Lord God.

The Bible is filled with stories of men and women who found great courage in the Lord. In some sense, those who demonstrated the most bravery are all considered brave because of their unwavering trust in the Lord. David knew he would be king, and so he had confidence in the face of death. David knew the Lord would not be mocked, so he had confidence in the face of the battle. Courage comes from an unwavering trust that God is in control of our lives. We may fight, but the battle belongs to the Lord.

Obedience breeds courage—in ourselves and in others. David was a lowly shepherd boy, probably not yet old enough to join Saul's army. This situation might have bothered him somewhat and made him feel left out, as his older brothers had gone off to fight the Philistines. But David had work of his own to do tending his father's sheep and carrying food and supplies to his brothers in battle. He did not become bitter or resentful in his role as errand boy. Instead, he attended faithfully to the mundane tasks his father asked him to do.

It was this very faithfulness that led David, quite unexpectedly, into a situation that required great courage—and it was this very faithfulness that bolstered his courage to face that challenge. He was already prepared to fight Goliath because he had already been faithful to his father's work. David had developed the habit of obeying immediately and completely, and that habit brought him the courage to answer Goliath's challenge. When the Israelites saw God had honored David's obedience, they responded by shaking off their fear and going into battle themselves. David's obedience bred courage in those around him.

Courage and obedience always go hand in hand. The more we obey the Word of God, the more we will discover that God is always reliable—and that gives us courage to trust Him more. Once we obey Him, our obedience encourages obedience in others around us, and even our smallest acts of courage breed courage in others as well.

REFLECTING ON THE TEXT

5) Why did the army of Israel tremble with fear? How could they have gained courage?

_____

_____

_____

_____

6) What was the source of David's courage? What was the source of Saul's cowardice? What was the fundamental difference between the two men?

_____

_____

_____

_____

7) What would the Israelites have thought if Saul had defeated Goliath? How does the Lord's use of David give Him more glory than if He had used Saul?

_____

_____

_____

_____

8) When have you acted on emotion rather than on faith? When have you acted on faith in spite of strong emotions? What were the results in each case?

_____

_____

_____

_____

PERSONAL RESPONSE

9) How do you ensure the Lord gets the glory for the accomplishments in your life?

_____

_____

_____

10) What steps of obedience is the Lord calling you to take this week? How might those steps increase your own courage? How might they increase courage in others?

_____

_____

_____

10

DAVID AND JONATHAN
1 Samuel 20:1–42

DRAWING NEAR

Consider a time you found yourself in the middle of a conflict that two or more of your friends were having. How did you handle the situation?

_____

_____

_____

THE CONTEXT

As today's passage opens, Saul, the near-mad king, was still holding the throne in Israel, but David had already been anointed as God's chosen ruler. This situation was naturally bringing a degree of conflict—a nation cannot have two kings, and one of the two men would have to go. Saul therefore set about getting rid of David in the vain hope that he could hold on to the kingship himself and pass it on to his son.

Meanwhile, David had been completely faithful to King Saul and was serving him valiantly as a soldier. Yet this only served to increase the tension for Saul as he became conflicted about whether to murder the young man who had been so devoted to him. Saul began to slip into dangerous instability, one minute swearing loyalty to David and the next minute throwing spears at his head.

Into this deadly situation stepped Jonathan, Saul's son and heir to the throne. Because David was Jonathan's main rival to the throne, one would expect Jonathan to take matters into his own hands and kill David himself. Jonathan was an important leader in Israel's army—a fighting man with great power and skill (see 1 Samuel 14). He would be the next king as long as David was not around.

But that is not what Jonathan chose to do. He knew the Lord had chosen David to be king, not him. So instead of joining Saul in his attempts to eliminate David, he opted to remain loyal to his closest friend. These two great men of valor shared a deep love for God, and that forged their devotion to each other.

Keys to the Text

Read 1 Samuel 20:1–42, noting the key words and phrases indicated below.

> DAVID SEEKS A FRIEND: *David's victories have made him popular with the people but unpopular with Saul. So the king sets out to kill David, prompting him to turn to his closest friend for help: Saul's oldest son, Jonathan.*

20:1. DAVID FLED: Saul had determined to murder David and tried to pin him against the wall with his spear, so David fled to Samuel. Saul sent men after him, but the Spirit of the Lord prevented them from capturing him. After a time, David took flight again to avoid Saul's men.

NAIOTH IN RAMAH: Perhaps dwellings or quarters within the town limits of Ramah, where Samuel and his company of prophets and disciples met for training, prayer, and fellowship.

JONATHAN: Jonathan was the eldest son of Saul and heir to the throne in Saul's mind. (The Israelites had already started to follow the ways of the world by assuming a king's son would become king in the future, which was not the Lord's plan.)

WHAT IS MY INIQUITY: David had done nothing to provoke Saul. On the contrary, he had done many things in loyal service. He had slain Goliath and led successful raiding parties against the Philistines. He was also the only person in Saul's court who could soothe the king's troubled spirits with his music. But Saul was still intent on killing him because David was the Lord's anointed king. Saul was losing his sanity in his determination to cling to power.

2. IT IS NOT SO: At this point, Jonathan was evidently unaware of Saul's intentions to murder David and apparently did not know that Saul had already thrown his spear at him. Saul had also sworn an oath to not kill David, and Jonathan fully trusted his father's word. In fact, his relationship with Saul appears to have been quite close, as he fully expected his father to take him into his confidence on matters of state. Jonathan's friendship with David had grown strong, but this situation threatened to put him in a difficult position. If Jonathan's father was in fact trying to kill David, he would have to choose where his deepest loyalties lay.

3. YOUR FATHER CERTAINLY KNOWS: The friendship between Jonathan and David added fuel to Saul's determination to kill David. This also added to Jonathan's difficult predicament: he loved his father dearly and was completely loyal to him, but he was also loyal to his friend David. Jonathan recognized that David was the legitimate heir to the throne because he had been anointed as such by God.

4. WHATEVER YOU YOURSELF DESIRE: Jonathan had a healthy respect for God's anointed. He recognized his final loyalty was to the Lord and not to any man, whether his father or his closest friend. David was God's anointed king, and Jonathan recognized his kingly authority.

A COVENANT OF FRIENDSHIP: David and Jonathan swear an oath of love and faithfulness. Both men will keep the oath until their dying day.

5. THE NEW MOON: The Israelites held a sacrificial meal on the first day of each month as a way of consecrating the month to the Lord. Saul, as king, would have rightfully expected David to be present at the meal.

6. A YEARLY SACRIFICE: Apparently, David's family held an annual family reunion that coincided with one of the monthly new moon celebrations.

7. IF HE IS VERY ANGRY: Saul's response would reveal the truth in his heart. If he cared for David, he would be happy to have him be with his family

for their annual gathering. But if he was consumed by envy, then he would become angry at David's absence. Saul wanted to know where David was at all times so he could kill him when the opportunity arose.

8. COVENANT: David and Jonathan had made a covenant of friendship (see 1 Samuel 18:1–3), and each loved the other like a brother. Both would remain true to their word throughout their lives, and David would even be faithful to it many years after Jonathan's death. It is important to recognize that Jonathan swore this oath to David before any trouble arose between David and Saul, yet Jonathan kept his word even after it became costly to do so.

KILL ME YOURSELF: As his covenant friend, David asked Jonathan to kill him if he was deserving of death because of his possible sin.

12. THE LORD GOD OF ISRAEL IS WITNESS: Here again we see the importance of keeping one's word. When a Christian commits to some course of action, he or she has made a commitment before the Lord.

SEND TO YOU AND TELL YOU: If Jonathan had good news for David, he would send a messenger to bring him back to court. But if Jonathan had bad news, he would go himself to tell David and send him away from court.

14. THAT I MAY NOT DIE: Jonathan recognized David would take the throne sooner or later because the Lord had already said it would be so. It was customary in those days for a new king to put to death any member of a previous king's family to ensure nobody could lay claim to the throne. Jonathan was asking David to not take such a step toward the family of Saul.

15. YOU SHALL NOT CUT OFF YOUR KINDNESS FROM MY HOUSE FOREVER: Jonathan may have suspected he would not be alive when David took the throne, so he asked for mercy on his descendants as well. One day, David would keep his promise, showing great kindness to Jonathan's son Mephibosheth, who was lame (see 2 Samuel 9).

WHEN THE LORD HAS CUT OFF EVERY ONE OF THE ENEMIES OF DAVID: Jonathan was a man of great faith and loyalty. He knew the Lord had chosen David, and he fully anticipated that David would become king and be established in Israel forever. There was no doubt in his mind that God's word would come to pass completely.

17. HE LOVED HIM AS HE LOVED HIS OWN SOUL: The friendship between Jonathan and David is an excellent model of the love that believers are to have toward one another. Each man was willing to sacrifice himself to protect

the other, as Jonathan's actions would soon prove. Each man loved the other as he loved himself, as Jesus commands us to do in Matthew 22:39.

HATCHING THE PLAN: Jonathan establishes a secret code by which he will tell David whether his life is in danger. He then returns to Saul's court to find out.

19. THE PLACE WHERE YOU HID ON THE DAY OF THE DEED: This may refer to the place where David hid when he first fled from Saul (see 1 Samuel 19:2).

STONE EZEL: Ezel may mean "departure stone." The location of this stone is unknown, but it was evidently a well-known landmark in the field where David would be hiding.

20. I WILL SHOOT THREE ARROWS: Jonathan's elaborate way of communicating the news to David was necessary if he was to keep David's location a secret. He could not even trust his own servants, lest Saul learn where David was hiding.

22. THE LORD HAS SENT YOU AWAY: Jonathan once again revealed his complete faith in the Lord's sovereignty. He viewed David's entire plight as part of God's plan.

25. ABNER: Saul's cousin and commander of his army.

26. HE IS UNCLEAN: Saul noticed David's absence immediately, but he initially assumed he was ritually unclean and unable to participate in the worship feast (see Leviticus 7:20–21).

28. DAVID EARNESTLY ASKED PERMISSION OF ME TO GO TO BETHLEHEM: We can assume that David spent the three days in Bethlehem with his family.

31. YOU SHALL NOT BE ESTABLISHED: Here we see a stark contrast between Jonathan and his father. Saul's chief concern was for his own political power, and he was outraged to discover Jonathan did not share that priority. As long as David was alive, Jonathan's succession to the throne was in jeopardy, and Saul's line would die with him. But Jonathan's heart was fixed on obeying God, even though it meant he would never become king.

SAUL'S REACTION: The king responds to his son's pleas by attempting to end Jonathan's life. At last Jonathan understands the truth of his father's intentions toward David.

33. SAUL CAST A SPEAR AT HIM TO KILL HIM: Saul's self-will was slowly driving him to insanity, and his anger was consuming him to the point he was

willing to murder his own son in a fit of rage to cling to his power. At this moment, Jonathan's eyes were opened to his father's true nature, and his conflict of loyalties was made clear.

38. MAKE HASTE, HURRY, DO NOT DELAY: As promised, Jonathan gave David the signal that he should leave the area and hide from Saul, but he added the loud proclamation that he must hurry, for his life was in imminent danger.

39. THE LAD DID NOT KNOW ANYTHING: Jonathan's caution proved wise, as he discovered for himself. Saul would stop at nothing to find David, and it might have been disastrous to permit a servant lad to know of Jonathan's communications.

41. BOWED DOWN THREE TIMES: David's bowing down more than once acknowledged Jonathan as the prince and expressed humble affection for him.

THEY WEPT TOGETHER: Both Jonathan and David were masculine men, seasoned warriors, and great leaders, yet they were not ashamed to display their masculine affection for one another with tears at their parting. This scene is deeply poignant, for it is unlikely the two friends were ever together again.

42. THE CITY: That is, Gibeah, the home of Saul. From this point until Saul's death, David was an outcast from the royal court.

UNLEASHING THE TEXT

1) Why was Saul trying to kill David? Why did Jonathan defend him?

_____

_____

_____

_____

_____

2) Why did Jonathan make such an elaborate ruse to find out whether Saul intended to kill David? What does this reveal about the danger Jonathan faced?

_____

_____

_____

3) If you had been in Jonathan's place, how would you have handled this difficult situation? What would you have done in David's place? In Saul's place?

_____

_____

_____

4) Why did David and Jonathan become such committed friends? What might have been the foundation of their friendship?

_____

_____

_____

EXPLORING THE MEANING

The Lord is pleased with those who are faithful. Jonathan and David were men of loyalty and faithfulness. Jonathan was loyal to his father, both as father and as king, and he was also loyal to David as friend and as future king. Both he and David were completely faithful to their word, and David kept his vow of friendship long after Jonathan had died.

Such faithfulness can often come with a cost. Jonathan was caught in a difficult situation where his loyalty to his father and his friend were in conflict. For David, as we will see in a later study, his faithfulness to the Lord's anointed prevented him from doing any harm to Saul, even though the king was actively trying to kill him. For Jonathan, the cost of faithfulness was the throne. As long as David was alive, he would never be king. The Scriptures are full of men and women who made faithfulness to God their highest priority, even at the cost of their own lives.

Hebrews 11 is filled with many heroes of the faith—men and women who placed their faith in God's word and demonstrated faithfulness to Him throughout their lives. "[They] were tortured, not accepting deliverance, that they might obtain a better resurrection. Still others had trial of mockings and scourgings, yes, and of chains and imprisonment. They were stoned, they were sawn in two, were tempted, were slain with the sword. They wandered about in sheepskins and goatskins, being destitute, afflicted, tormented" (Hebrews 11:35–37). The Bible says the world was not worthy of them. God is pleased with those who remain faithful to Him.

God does not promise long life or material prosperity. Jonathan was a man after God's own heart, just as David was, yet both men suffered injustice and hardship. Jonathan would die young in battle, dutifully standing by his father, the king. David had been anointed by Samuel to take the throne of Israel, yet he was forced to run for his life for many years. He hid in caves, lived with Israel's enemies, and even feigned madness once in order to save his own life—yet he was faithful to the word of God.

The Lord does not promise that His people will be exempt from suffering or hardship or sorrows. In fact, quite the opposite is true: those who follow Christ must expect to share in His sorrows just as we share in His glory. David and other saints of Scripture understood this principle, so they did not lose heart when suffering came their way. Paul, for example, spent many years in various Roman prisons, even though his deep desire was to be traveling the world as a missionary. Yet his imprisonment led to a large portion of our New Testament.

God's people must not lose heart when suffering comes, for the Lord uses all things in our lives—both good and bad—to perfect His character in us. "My brethren, count it all joy when you fall into various trials, knowing that the testing of your faith produces patience. But let patience have its perfect work, that you may be perfect and complete, lacking nothing" (James 1:2–4).

Devotion to God outweighs the riches of the world. Jonathan was the son of a king, and that position of honor brought with it many aspects of power and wealth. From the world's eyes, he was heir to the throne of Israel, and the entire army was at his command to protect that inheritance. His father, in fact, was actively working to remove Jonathan's sole "rival" to the throne. All Jonathan needed to do was cooperate with Saul's plan to kill David, and his inheritance would have been (in Saul's thinking) fully secure.

But Jonathan cared nothing for the world's temporary advancements and fading glories. He understood that the earth's kingdoms will all pass away and only love shall remain—and he invested his future in his love for David. He was willing to sacrifice all the great honors that were his by birth, and he even risked his life to help David ascend the very throne that might have been his own. Saul chose to love his own legacy (and even his son) more than God. Jonathan esteemed the Lord's choice for king far ahead of his own interests.

Jesus says, "If anyone comes to Me and does not hate his father and mother, wife and children, brothers and sisters, yes, and his own life also, he cannot be My disciple" (Luke 14:26). Christians are called to choose faithfulness to God over their own desires and even over their families. This was a decision Saul was not willing to make, but one that Jonathan and David made gladly, knowing the glories of serving God outweigh anything this world has to offer.

REFLECTING ON THE TEXT

5) In what ways was Jonathan's friendship to David costly to himself? What does this reveal about his character?

_____

_____

_____

6) Why did David and Jonathan make a covenant of friendship? On what was this covenant based? What pressures and situations were threatening their friendship?

_____

_____

_____

_____

_____

_____

7) What does it mean that Jonathan loved David "as he loved his own soul"? How would such a love be demonstrated in practical terms?

_____

_____

_____

_____

8) Even in their friendship, David and Jonathan loved God more than each other. How did they demonstrate this? Give some examples from their words and deeds.

_____

_____

_____

_____

PERSONAL RESPONSE

9) In what areas do you find yourself putting your own interests above those of others? How do your friendships show the supremacy of God, as David and Jonathan's did?

_____

_____

_____

10) What areas of faithfulness need strengthening in your life? What commitments do you need to honor this week?

_____

_____

_____

11

SAUL'S FINAL DAYS
1 Samuel 24:1–22; 28:1–20

DRAWING NEAR

Think of a time in your life where you chose to be merciful to someone who had wronged you when you could have easily taken revenge. What enabled you to take that course of action?

_____

_____

_____

THE CONTEXT

David was now on the run, hiding from King Saul and his men anywhere he could find. He first fled to the tabernacle at Nob, where he retrieved Goliath's sword. From there he fled into enemy territory, feigning madness so the Philistine king would not kill him. He then assembled a small group of fighting men to accompany him—some four hundred who had left Israel for their own reasons. David led that fighting band against the Philistines, and the Lord gave him great success (see 1 Samuel 21–23).

Yet nothing David did alleviated Saul's hatred. The king pursued him day after day throughout the wilderness in hopes of putting him to death once and for all. This was taxing on David, to say the least, and on his men as well.

They were forced to live in caves and woodlands, foraging for supplies and constantly running from one place to the next. They could not remain in any one location for too long because they knew that even the Israelites themselves could betray them to Saul.

Then one day, when David and his men were hiding in a cave, the Lord delivered Saul into his hand. David was given the perfect opportunity to finally end this madness. After all, wasn't he already anointed king of Israel? If anyone had the right to slay an attacker, it was the persecuted and legitimate king of Israel. But David stayed his hand and refused to do any harm to Saul because he was intent on respecting the one the Lord had anointed as king.

In this study, we will examine this episode of faithfulness on David's part. We will also witness another tragic event near the end of Saul's life in which he chose to completely turn his back on God and seek guidance from the devil. The man who had been anointed by God and transformed into a prophet would finish out his days frightened and alone. It was a sad end to what could have been an incredible life of faithfulness to God.

KEYS TO THE TEXT

Read 1 Samuel 24:1–22, noting the key words and phrases indicated below.

> SAUL HUNTS DAVID: *Saul takes some time off from fighting the Philistines to pursue his obsession: trying to kill David.*

24:1. SAUL HAD RETURNED FROM FOLLOWING THE PHILISTINES: Saul's kingship was marked by constant fighting against the Philistines, and the nation knew few times of peace during his reign. It was not until well into David's reign that the Philistine menace was quelled once and for all.

DAVID IS IN THE WILDERNESS OF EN GEDI: As important as the Philistine threat was to Saul, there was another priority that was higher still: killing David. Many times Saul set aside what he was doing to pursue David, forcing David to flee from one location to another just to stay alive.

2. DAVID AND HIS MEN: By this time, David had assembled a small fighting band of his own composed of men who had their own reasons for fleeing Israel—and most of them not very good reasons. He had gathered some four

hundred men, "everyone who was in distress, everyone who was in debt, and everyone who was discontented" (1 Samuel 22:2). David's men were unskilled warriors (though they were becoming more skilled as time passed), while Saul went after them with three thousand elite troops. David was outnumbered and underequipped.

ROCKS OF THE WILD GOATS: David was reduced to living in caves and atop wild crags, moving constantly to stay alive. He was the legitimate king of Israel, yet he lived as an outlaw in the most uncomfortable and perilous conditions.

NATURE CALLS: Saul uses a cave to relieve himself, but he does not realize David is hiding inside. This is David's big chance to kill his enemy.

3. SAUL WENT IN TO ATTEND TO HIS NEEDS: The literal phrase is that Saul went into the cave to "cover his feet." He would have been crouching in a corner with his inner garment dropped to his feet. He was in a vulnerable position, and David's fighters were hidden right nearby.

4. THIS IS THE DAY: Here we find David faced with a difficult decision. The Lord had anointed him as king, and Samuel had told him that he would rule Israel, so it must have seemed like divine providence for Saul to be delivered into his hand this way. Yet David also knew that Saul had been anointed by the Lord at one time. Although Saul had since been rejected as king, David recognized it was not his place to raise his hand against the Lord's anointed— even when that anointed one had fallen away from God.

5. DAVID'S HEART TROUBLED HIM: David was so determined to respect the Lord's anointed that he even felt guilty for cutting off a piece of Saul's robe—though that piece of robe would prove he had shown respect for Saul and win him a season of peace.

7. DAVID RESTRAINED HIS SERVANTS: God had also anointed David to be king, and as such he took seriously his responsibility for those under his care. This concept cuts both ways: we are all called to respect those whom God has placed in authority over us, but we are also held accountable for those under our leadership. David recognized that if his men attacked Saul, he would be held accountable since they were under his authority.

David Confronts Saul: David holds great respect for the Lord's anointed, but that does not mean he pretends that evil is good. He confronts Saul with his sin.

8. My lord the king: Notice the deep respect David showed to Saul, bowing himself to the ground and addressing him as "my lord." This was a remarkable way for David to respond to the man who had been trying to murder him without any cause. David's words must have smitten Saul's conscience— especially when one considers that, had the tables been turned, Saul would not have hesitated to kill David.

10. the Lord delivered you today into my hand: David's men saw the opportunity as the Lord's way of delivering Saul into their hands, but David saw it as his opportunity to demonstrate humility and obedience to the Lord's will. Here is an example of the way David was a man after God's own heart; he saw the events of life from the Lord's perspective rather than from that of the world.

11. there is neither evil nor rebellion in my hand: From a legal perspective, David might have been justified in killing Saul because Saul was trying to kill him. But David's view was that the Lord had allowed Saul to hunt him, and the Lord would be faithful to remove the threat when His time was right. In the meantime, David saw any armed resistance to Saul as an act of rebellion. His defense was in the Lord, and he would not raise his hand against Saul.

12. Let the Lord judge between you and me: Yet David did not gloss over the terrible deeds of Saul. He did not that pretend Saul was a good king or that he had some sort of divine right to murder him. His reason for not fighting back was to be submissive to God's will, but he did not hesitate to ask the Lord to judge the wickedness he was enduring.

13. Wickedness proceeds from the wicked: This is as close as David came to rebuking Saul. He did not feel it was his place to openly defy the king, but he also was willing to clearly state an important principle: our actions define our character. Those who act wickedly are wicked, but David would define his own character by not retaliating.

16. Saul lifted up his voice and wept: Saul was confronted with his own wickedness simply by the contrast of David's righteousness.

22. DAVID SWORE TO SAUL: Saul had sworn on more than one occasion that he would not kill David. Unlike Saul, David would keep his oath.

Read 1 Samuel 28:1–20, noting the key words and phrases indicated below.

THE LAST DAYS OF KING SAUL: We now fast-forward to the last day of Saul's life. Saul was in yet another battle with the Philistines, and he was outnumbered, surrounded, and desperate.

28:1. THE PHILISTINES GATHERED THEIR ARMIES: We are now near Saul's tragic end.

ACHISH: David had again fled to the Philistine city of Gath, ruled by Achish. This put him in a delicate situation, as the Philistines expected him to fight on their behalf against Israel.

3. SAUL HAD PUT THE MEDIUMS AND THE SPIRITISTS OUT OF THE LAND: In Israel, those who practiced occult arts were to be put to death (see Leviticus 20:27). God hates witchcraft in any form, because the occult is the realm of Satan. Those who dabble in it are making themselves available to the devil and his minions. Saul understood this and had obeyed the Word of God—to a point. Yet his own self-interests always trumped God's Word.

5. HE WAS AFRAID: Once again, we see that David was a man of courage while Saul was a man of timidity. The difference between the two lay not in some character trait but in their respective views of God. Saul's final authority was his own will and expedience, and he therefore trusted in his own might. David's strength, however, was in the Lord, and the Lord delivered him from all his enemies. This battle against the Philistines was to be Saul's last.

6. THE LORD DID NOT ANSWER HIM: What a terrible ending after such a promising beginning! The Lord had once inhabited Saul through the power of His Holy Spirit, but now He would not even answer his call.

SAUL AND THE WITCH: Saul's last act as king is to consult a medium, thus turning his back fully on the Lord. Ironically, both Saul and the medium are terrified when Samuel actually appears.

7. FIND ME A WOMAN WHO IS A MEDIUM: Saul revealed his true heart in this moment of crisis by turning away from God and toward the devil in

order to meet his own needs. It is interesting to note that Saul's servant knew exactly where to find such a medium in the land, even though witchcraft had been outlawed in Israel.

8. SAUL DISGUISED HIMSELF: Saul found himself in a snare of his own making. He had banned witches from the land, yet he now was seeking their service. In order to accomplish this, he decided to dress up and hope the witch would not see who he really was.

10. SAUL SWORE TO HER BY THE LORD: The hypocrisy of this oath was breathtaking. Saul had completely abandoned any pretense of obeying the commands of the Lord and had deliberately turned to demonic sources for guidance—yet he persisted in his outward appearances of godliness by invoking the Lord in his oath.

12. SHE CRIED OUT WITH A LOUD VOICE: There is a certain bitter humor in this picture. The witch did not expect to have a real human spirit appear before her, because her craft was drawn from the powers of hell. Mediums cannot talk with "departed spirits"; they can only connect with the unseen and fallen spirit beings that follow the devil. This witch may also have been a charlatan who was accustomed to deceiving her customers with phony mumbo jumbo, as many do today. Either way, she did not expect Samuel himself to appear before her.

15. WHY HAVE YOU DISTURBED ME: It is important to recognize that mankind cannot contact those who have died. There are people who claim to do so, but those people are either outright frauds or, much worse, holding communication with demons. In this one case, however, it appears the Lord permitted the spirit of Samuel to appear before Saul. There is no other event like this anywhere in Scripture.

I AM DEEPLY DISTRESSED: This was always Saul's excuse for disobeying the Word of God. Yet he himself had caused much deep distress in the life of David, and David had still remained faithful to God. The difference lay within the will of each man. It is not enough to perform an outward display of religion; we must also set our wills and our hearts to obedience, even when we are "deeply distressed."

16. THE LORD HAS . . . BECOME YOUR ENEMY: There can be no words more terrifying than these. If the Lord turns His back on a person, there is no further recourse—no source of mercy, truth, or life itself.

UNLEASHING THE TEXT

1) Why did David choose not to kill Saul? What does this show about his understanding of God's control of Israel?

_____

_____

_____

2) If you had been in David's situation with Saul in the cave, what would you have done? How would you have responded if you'd been in Saul's situation?

_____

_____

_____

3) Why did Saul feel he needed to consult a witch? What would it have taken at this point to restore his relationship with the Lord?

_____

_____

_____

4) Why did God refuse to answer Saul's prayers at the end of his life? What does this teach us about how prayer works?

_____

_____

_____

EXPLORING THE MEANING

Do not revile those who persecute you. David had been the only Israelite willing to stand up to Goliath, and he had wrought a great victory for Saul's army. He was the only person who could soothe Saul when the evil spirit persecuted him. Even after Saul had driven him out of his court, David continued to lead raids against the Philistines and help Saul protect Israel against its enemies. Yet in spite of all his faithful service, David suffered under a constant threat of murder and was frequently betrayed by his own people.

If ever there were a person who had a right to speak harshly to his persecutor, it was David. But when he confronted Saul—even after sparing Saul's life when others wanted to kill him—he still did not revile his enemy. He respected Saul's position as king and bowed with his face to the ground. He did not pretend that Saul was not sinning against him, but he spoke the truth to the king in a humble fashion.

This can be a hard lesson for us to learn, but it is important if we are to be like Christ. The injustices against David pale in significance to those heaped on Jesus. The holy Son of God—who had *never* sinned—submitted Himself quietly to the scourging and mockery of His tormentors. As Peter would later write, "Christ also suffered for us, leaving us an example, that you should follow His steps: 'Who committed no sin, nor was deceit found in His mouth'; who, when He was reviled, did not revile in return; when He suffered, He did not threaten, but committed Himself to Him who judges righteously" (1 Peter 2:21–23).

Sin produces self-deception. There are numerous ironies in Saul's encounter with the witch. Saul had banned witches from the land, but then felt he needed to use one. Saul had to wear a disguise so the witch would not fear legal punishment for engaging in a practice that he himself had banned. The whole incident begs the question that if Saul thought the witch had actual insight, why didn't he fear she would see through his disguise? The final irony is seen in the witch's surprise when the prophet Samuel responded. It is clear this was the first time she had actually been successful.

All of these ironies show how self-deceived both Saul and the witch were. She knew her practice was a hoax, but she persisted in it anyway. Saul knew witches had no real power, but he went to one for guidance anyway. Finally, Saul explained away his obvious disobedience by saying the Lord would not answer his prayers, which is why he needed Samuel—or at least a witch. Yet Samuel saw through that self-deception and told Saul the issue was his sin, not the Lord's punishment.

As long as Saul was God's enemy, he would receive no answer to his prayers. Yet he was so self-deceived that even after seeing Samuel and receiving the prophecy that he would lose the battle and die that day, he refused to repent. The witch brought him his last meal, and he returned to the battle—as blinded by sin as he was when he first put on his disguise.

God uses even wicked people for His purposes. Saul did not apply to be king. He did not lobby for the job. The Lord chose him for it, and He did so because He wanted to give Israel what they deserved. The Israelites wanted a king so they could be like the other nations, so God chose a king who was just like the other nations' kings.

The Holy Spirit empowered Saul at the beginning of his reign, and Israel was victorious. But when Saul chose to love himself rather than the Lord, the Spirit left him. From that moment on, the only victories Israel had were under David's leadership. By the end of Saul's life, Israel was being decimated by their enemies, and Saul's ego had placed his own pride above Israel's well-being. In short, Israel was getting exactly what they asked for and exactly what they deserved. Saul spent his life fighting against the Lord's purposes, but in the end, his whole life was spent fulfilling those very same purposes.

This same dynamic is seen in the death of Jesus. His biggest enemies—Judas, Pilate, and the Pharisees—all committed the greatest sin imaginable by crucifying the Son of God. Yet it was that sinful act that brought about God's plan of salvation for His children. Even the wicked are used by the Lord for His own purposes.

REFLECTING ON THE TEXT

5) How do you respond to those who abuse their authority? How did David respond? How did Jesus respond?

_____

_____

_____

6) Why did God allow Saul to persecute David for so long? What was He teaching Saul? What was He teaching David? What was He teaching the nation of Israel?

_____

_____

_____

7) What was Saul's response to Samuel's dire warning? Is this what you expected from him? How is it in keeping with his character?

_____

_____

_____

8) How did God use Saul's life for His purposes? How did Samuel's prophecy in 1 Samuel 8:11–18 prove to be true in Israel's first experience with a king?

_____

_____

_____

_____

PERSONAL RESPONSE

9) In what ways do you struggle with a rebellious spirit? In what areas might the Lord be calling you to be more submissive to Him?

_____

_____

_____

10) How have you responded recently to people who have treated you badly? How can you imitate the humility of Christ this week?

_____

_____

_____

12

REVIEWING KEY PRINCIPLES

DRAWING NEAR

As you look back at each of the studies in 1 Samuel, what is the one thing that stood out to you the most? What is one new perspective you have learned?

_____

_____

_____

THE CONTEXT

We have covered an important period in the history of Israel during this study. We watched as the nation moved from the leadership of judges to a king. We have seen some great contrasts in the characters. Some, such as Samuel, had a close walk with God, while others, like Eli, didn't really know Him at all. Some, like David, possessed great courage, while others, like Saul, were riddled with constant fear. Yet one theme has remained constant throughout these studies: *God is faithful*, and those who obey Him will grow in faithfulness as well.

The fruits of godly faithfulness are many. One such fruit is loyalty, as seen in the profound friendship between Jonathan and David, which lasted more than a lifetime. Another is respect, which David showed for Saul's position as God's anointed. These things come from obedience to God's Word, not from within oneself. Saul strove to find power in his own will, while Samuel and David found their strength in the character of God.

Here are a few of the major principles we have found during our study. There are many more we don't have room to reiterate, so take some time to review the earlier studies—or, better still, to meditate on the passages of Scripture that we have covered. As you do, ask the Holy Spirit to give you wisdom and insight into His Word. He will not refuse.

EXPLORING THE MEANING

The Lord is pleased by a willing heart. Samuel was scarcely more than a boy, certainly no older than fourteen, when he heard a voice in the deep watches of the night calling his name. He leaped out of bed without complaining and rushed to his master—only to find Eli had not called him. When he heard the voice a second time, he did not lie in bed and ignore it; he ran once again to Eli's side. When the Lord gave him some bad news for Eli, his heart quaked at the thought of delivering such a message to the man who was like a father to him, yet he did so in obedience to the Lord—and he delivered it in full.

Eli, on the other hand, served the Lord less willingly. When he was faced with the unpleasant task of disciplining his sons, he did not obey fully but only halfheartedly. Samuel's quick and willing obedience, even in unpleasant tasks, stood as a tacit rebuke to the high priest. We saw the same contrast between Saul and David.

The Lord does not want His people to serve Him grudgingly but willingly and cheerfully. Jesus said, "Take My yoke upon you and learn from Me, for I am gentle and lowly in heart, and you will find rest for your souls. For My yoke is easy and My burden is light" (Matthew 11:29–30). And 2 Chronicles 16:9 tells us that "the eyes of the LORD run to and fro throughout the whole earth, to show Himself strong on behalf of those whose heart is loyal to Him."

Serving the Lord requires obedience to His Word. We see this principle at work in the life of Eli, who served the Lord at the temple in Shiloh for forty years and even acted as one of Israel's last judges. He had risen to the highest level in the priestly class and achieved the greatest honor and responsibility a Levite could obtain. Yet in the end it was all in vain, and he died literally as a broken man.

This principle was also at work in the lives of the men of Beth Shemesh. The Philistines' mistreatment of the ark, the holy symbol of the Lord, brought devastation on the people as long as it was in their hands. We would expect to see something different when the ark was returned to God's people, but when the men committed the sin of presumption, they were struck down just as the Philistines had been.

The men's question, "Who is able to stand before this holy LORD God?" (1 Samuel 6:20), emphasizes this point. The Lord required obedience to His Word, and that applied to both those who were inside and outside His covenant. Knowing God is not an intellectual exercise but a spiritual devotion that comes from submitting ourselves to Him as Savior and obeying Him as Lord. Eli and the men of Beth Shemesh did not live in obedience to God's Word, and we must take care to not repeat their mistake.

The Lord gives victory in the battle. The Philistines were a powerful nation, and their armies were feared throughout Canaan. The Israelites were armed with slings and bows at best, and many fought with simple farm tools. They were no match for the iron weapons and chariots of the mighty Philistines, and their hearts were filled with fear when the enemy gathered in force on their borders.

But their powerful foe could not stand before the wrath of God, and He sent them into confusion simply by roaring out with a thunderous voice. The Israelites still had to participate in the battle on that occasion, just as the Lord still involves His people in spiritual warfare today, but ultimately the victory belonged to Him alone. God's people still face many foes today, whether from the open hostility of the world or from spiritual attacks of Satan. Yet the principle still applies: the Lord will defend and protect His people, and He can never lose.

It is important to remember what God has done for us in the past, most notably in the sacrifice of His own Son on the cross at Calvary. As the apostle Paul rhetorically asks, "If God is for us, who can be against us? He who did not spare His own Son, but delivered Him up for us all, how shall He not with Him also freely give us all things?" (Romans 8:31–32).

We are to follow God, not imitate the world. The nation of Israel was surrounded by pagan nations, many of whom were wealthy and powerful. It would have been easy for them to look at their Philistine neighbors and envy their prosperity and military power, and easier still to become tempted by the carnal practices seen in their pagan temples. The people may even have justified such envy with the attitude that, if the Philistines prospered by serving Baal, it couldn't be all that bad!

In order to imitate another person, we must pay close attention to that person. In order to imitate the Canaanites, the Israelites had to focus their eyes on their neighbors—and that meant taking their eyes *off* their God. What we focus on becomes our role model. If we immerse ourselves in the entertainments and lifestyles of the world, we will end up imitating the world.

Christians are to immerse themselves in the Word of God, regular corporate worship, and prayer. When we fill our hearts and minds with the presence and Word of God, our eyes will be steadfastly focused on Christ—and we will find ourselves imitating Him. As Paul writes, "Therefore be imitators of God as dear children. And walk in love, as Christ also has loved us and given Himself for us, an offering and a sacrifice to God for a sweet-smelling aroma. But fornication and all uncleanness or covetousness, let it not even be named among you, as is fitting for saints; neither filthiness, nor foolish talking, nor coarse jesting, which are not fitting, but rather giving of thanks" (Ephesians 5:1–4).

God demands obedience, not expedience. Saul obeyed the Lord's commands as far as they suited his purposes. He attacked the Philistines in an effort to throw off their yoke of bondage, which was in obedience to the Lord's will. But when the battle became difficult, he did not hesitate to violate the Lord's commands by usurping the authority of God's chosen priests. He attacked the Amalekites and put the people to the sword, but he kept the chosen wealth and plunder for himself.

Both of these decisions might be seen in the world's eyes as simple expedience. Saul was in an emergency with the Philistines surrounding him, and Samuel was nowhere to be found. It was simply expedient for him to offer the sacrifices himself. Defeating the Amalekites was sufficient obedience; slaughtering good sheep would have been wasteful. But in both cases, Saul only obeyed in part—and he felt the freedom to choose for himself exactly *which* part to obey.

The Lord expects His people to obey fully, not in part. Difficult circumstances do not excuse us from obedience to the Lord's commands. The Christian's job is to obey God's Word and leave the consequences in His hands. The Lord had not abandoned Saul when the Philistines surrounded him, and had Saul waited for Samuel, the Lord would have worked a miraculous deliverance for Israel. He has not changed since Saul's time—He will deliver His people from destruction, yet He expects His people to obey His Word.

Man looks at the outward appearance, but the Lord looks at the heart. When Saul was anointed king, the qualities the people noticed were that he was tall and strong, standing head and shoulders above his peers. When Samuel met the sons of Jesse, he was immediately taken by the eldest son because he too was tall, strong, and very handsome.

Humans tend to believe the evidence of their senses, which is unavoidable to some extent because we live in a physical world that is experienced through those five senses. But God transcends the things of this material world, and He does not see our lives through five physical senses. God looks on the hearts of people, not on their outward appearances. He sees beyond our actions and accomplishments, weighing our hearts and looking for people who are determined to obey His Word.

It is interesting that the New Testament gives us no physical description of what Jesus looked like—how tall He was or what color His eyes were. The prophet Isaiah even tells us that "He has no form or comeliness; and when we see Him, there is no beauty that we should desire Him" (Isaiah 53:2). The Lord is not interested in such matters; He is concerned with whether we reflect the *heart* of Christ, devoting ourselves to obedience and faithfulness. That should be the focus of all God's people.

God receives glory from using those who trust Him. The main point of David's encounter with Goliath is that God can use even the most overmatched person for His glory. David did not win the battle because he had more courage than Goliath. Rather, he won the battle because the Lord was on his side. God could have sent His Spirit to empower Saul as he did in 1 Samuel 10, but then the glory for the victory would have gone to Saul. By using David, the Lord alone received the honor for the victory.

David knew this. While Saul was timid about becoming king, David rushed into battle trusting the Lord. While Saul continually thought that unless he acted a certain way he would lose his battles, David knew the battle was not his to lose. If David was on God's side, God would get the glory for the victory. Saul spent his life angry because God was not on his side. David spent his life with courage, knowing he was on the side of the Lord. For this reason, the Lord would get the praise because He was the one who achieved the victory.

"Blessed is the man who trusts in the LORD, and whose hope is the LORD. For he shall be like a tree planted by the waters, which spreads out its roots by the river, and will not fear when heat comes" (Jeremiah 17:7–8).

The Lord is pleased with those who are faithful. Jonathan and David were men of loyalty and faithfulness. Jonathan was loyal to his father, both as father and as king, and he was also loyal to David as friend and as the future king. Both he and David were completely faithful to their word, and David kept his vow of friendship long after Jonathan had died.

Such faithfulness can often come with a cost. Jonathan was caught in a difficult situation where his loyalty to his father and his friend were in conflict. For David, his faithfulness to the Lord's anointed prevented him from doing any harm to Saul, even though Saul was actively trying to kill him. For Jonathan, the cost of his faithfulness was the throne; as long as David was alive, Jonathan would never be king. The Scriptures are full of men and women who made faithfulness to God their highest priority, even at the cost of their own lives.

Hebrews 11 is filled with many heroes of the faith—men and women who placed their faith in God's word and demonstrated faithfulness to Him throughout their lives. "[They] were tortured, not accepting deliverance, that they might obtain a better resurrection. Still others had trial of mockings and scourgings, yes, and of chains and imprisonment. They were stoned, they were sawn in two, were tempted, were slain with the sword. They wandered about in sheepskins and goatskins, being destitute, afflicted, tormented." The Bible says the world was not worthy of them. God is pleased with those who remain faithful to Him.

Unleashing the Text

1) Which of the concepts or principles in this study have you found to be the most encouraging? Why?

_____

_____

_____

2) Which of the concepts or principles have you found most challenging? Why?

_____

_____

_____

3) What aspects of "walking with God" are you already obeying in your life? Which areas need strengthening?

_____

_____

_____

4) To which of the characters that we've studied have you most been able to relate? How might you emulate that person in your own life?

_____

_____

_____

PERSONAL RESPONSE

5) Have you taken a definite stand for Jesus Christ? Have you accepted His free gift of salvation? If not, what is preventing you from doing so?

_____

_____

_____

6) In what areas of your life have you been most convicted during this study? What exact things will you do to address these convictions? Be specific.

_____

_____

_____

7) What have you learned about the character of God during this study? How has this insight affected your worship or prayer life?

_____

_____

_____

8) What are some specific things you want to see God do in your life in the coming month? What are some things you intend to change in your own life during that time? (Return to this list in one month and hold yourself accountable to fulfill these things.)

_____

_____

_____

If you would like to continue in your study of the Old Testament, read the next title in this series: *2 Samuel: David's Heart Revealed.*

ALSO AVAILABLE

I n this study, John MacArthur guides readers through an in-depth look at the historical period beginning with God's calling of Moses, continuing through the giving of the Ten Commandments, and concluding with the Israelites' preparations to enter the Promised Land. This study includes close-up examinations of Aaron, Caleb, Joshua, Balaam and Balak, as well as careful considerations of doctrinal themes such as "Complaints and Rebellion" and "Following God's Law."

The MacArthur Bible Studies provide intriguing examinations of the whole of Scripture. Each guide incorporates extensive commentary, detailed observations on overriding themes, and probing questions to help you study the Word of God with guidance from John MacArthur.

Also Available

In this study, John MacArthur guides readers through an in-depth look at the Israelites' conquest of the Promised Land, beginning with the miraculous parting of the Jordan River, continuing through the victories and setbacks as the people settled into Canaan, and concluding with the time of the judges. Studies include close-up examinations of Rahab, Ruth, and Samson, as well as careful considerations of doctrinal themes such as "The Sin of Achan" and the role of "The Kinsman Redeemer."

The MacArthur Bible Studies provide intriguing examinations of the whole of Scripture. Each guide incorporates extensive commentary, detailed observations on overriding themes, and probing questions to help you study the Word of God with guidance from John MacArthur.

ALSO AVAILABLE

In this study, John MacArthur guides readers through an in-depth look at the historical period beginning with David's struggle to establish his throne, continuing through his sin and repentance, and concluding with the tragic rebellion of his son Absalom. Studies include close-up examinations of Joab, Amnon, Tamar, Absalom, and others, as well as careful considerations of doctrinal themes such as "Obedience and Blessing" and being a "Man After God's Own Heart."

The MacArthur Bible Studies provide intriguing examinations of the whole of Scripture. Each guide incorporates extensive commentary, detailed observations on overriding themes, and probing questions to help you study the Word of God with guidance from John MacArthur.

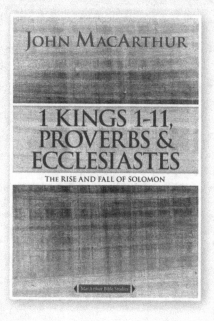

JOHN MACARTHUR

1 KINGS 1-11, PROVERBS & ECCLESIASTES

THE RISE AND FALL OF SOLOMON

MacArthur Bible Studies

In this study, John MacArthur guides readers through an in-depth look at the historical period beginning with Solomon's ascent to the throne and continuing through his tragic end. Studies include close-up examinations of the vital importance of wisdom—with portraits of the wise woman, the foolish sluggard, and others in the book of Proverbs—and careful considerations of doctrinal themes such as "True Wisdom from God" and "A Time for Everything."

The MacArthur Bible Studies provide intriguing examinations of the whole of Scripture. Each guide incorporates extensive commentary, detailed observations on overriding themes, and probing questions to help you study the Word of God with guidance from John MacArthur.